Merthyr Mawr bridge.

Shire County Guide 31

GLAMORGAN

John B. Hilling

Shire Publications Ltd

CONTENTS

1. Glamorgan: its landscape and history 3
2. Coast and countryside 7
3. Places of archaeological interest 13
4. Castles and monastic ruins 18
5. Churches and chapels 26
6. Historic houses and gardens 35
7. Museums 41
8. Industrial history 46
9. Other places to visit 55
10. Famous people 58
11. Cardiff 63
12. Towns and villages 66
13. Tourist information centres 77
    Map of Glamorgan 78
    Index 80

Shire Publications Ltd, Cromwell House, Church Street, Princes Risborough, Buckinghamshire HP17 9AJ, UK.

Printed in Great Britain by C. I. Thomas & Sons (Haverfordwest) Ltd, Press Buildings, Merlins Bridge, Haverfordwest, Dyfed SA61 1XF.

British Library Cataloguing in Publication Data: Hilling, John B. (John Bryan). Glamorgan. 1. Glamorgan (Wales). I. Title. 914. 429704859. ISBN 0-7478-0109-6.

ACKNOWLEDGEMENTS
Photographs are acknowledged as follows: Cadw: Welsh Historic Monuments, cover and pages 16, 17, 18, 23, 28, 35 and 36; Cardiff City Council, page 19; Glamorgan Gwent Archaeological Trust, pages 14, 17 and 53 (top); T. Herridge, page 30 (bottom); Cadbury Lamb, page 77. J. McNamara, pages 20, 41, 64 and 65; National Monuments Record (Royal Commission on Ancient Monuments Wales), pages 22, 30 (top), 40 and 51; Swansea City Council, pages 5 and 57; John Thomas, pages 3, 33, 38, 46, 48, 49 and 52; Welsh Tourist Board, pages 10, 45, 56 and 71; West Glamorgan County Council, page 39; M. Woodward of Terence Soames (Cardiff) Limited, page 63. The remaining photographs are by the author. The map is by Robert Dizon.

NOTES
Cadw is the state authority responsible for the care of ancient monuments and historic buildings in Wales.
    The locations of many of the places described in this book are identified by means of the national grid reference, given in the form of the two grid letters (denoting the 100 km square) and six figures, locating the site to within 100 metres. Each reference is preceded by the number of the Ordnance Survey (OS) Landranger map on which the place will be found: for example, OS 171: ST 143804. A full explanation of how to use grid references will be found on the Landranger maps.

Cover: *Castell Coch.*

Below: *Pennard Castle from Three Cliffs Bay.*

New Tredegar.

1
Glamorgan: its landscape and history

Glamorgan is the most populous and southerly part of Wales. Administratively it consists of three counties because in 1974, under local government reorganisation, the old county of Glamorgan was subdivided into Mid Glamorgan, mostly covering the Valleys, South Glamorgan, with its headquarters in Cardiff, and West Glamorgan, centred on Swansea; but as none of them is large they are treated as a single geographical county for the purpose of this volume. Glamorgan divides naturally into three distinct physical zones: the Vale of Glamorgan, or *Bro Morgannwg* as it was traditionally known; the Gower peninsula; and the uplands or *Blaenau*.

Physical regions

The **Vale of Glamorgan** is the lowland area bordering the southern coast and stretches from Cardiff westwards to Port Talbot. It is not a valley as the name implies but rather an undulating plain of limestone and younger rocks which have been uplifted to form a low plateau ending abruptly in a long line of cliffs at the coast. The Vale is drained by a few minor rivers and is generally fertile farmland although at its western end it is overlain by extensive sand dunes. Its small nucleated villages and the general absence of mountains are more suggestive of the scenery of lowland England than that of the Celtic west.

In many ways the **Gower peninsula,** lying between Swansea Bay and Carmarthen Bay at the western end of Glamorgan, is similar to the Vale, but, with no through roads and no major settlements, it is more isolated. Because of its superb coastal scenery most of the peninsula has been declared an Area of Outstanding Natural Beauty. As one travels west from Mumbles Head the rugged southern coast becomes progressively wilder and more dramatic. The northern coast of the peninsula is more subdued, its denuded old cliffs being some way inland behind a foreshore of marshes and saltings.

The **Blaenau** is hill country lying between the Brecon Beacons to the north and the Vale to the south. It comprises long moorland ridges of Pennant sandstone divided by parallel lines of valleys – the much maligned coalmining 'Valleys' of southern Wales. Until the coming of industry these valleys must have had an idyllic appearance. Now they have been largely filled with long lines of terrace housing and industry, but fortunately the steep valley sides have forced a limit on urban sprawl and there are still many delightful gaps between the mining townships. In places, such as the upper end of the Rhondda valley, the mountain scenery is almost alpine in its grandeur and waterfalls abound where the fast-flowing streams cross the encircling crest of carboniferous limestone.

Early man in Glamorgan

Man has been living in Glamorgan for many thousands of years. Indeed, the earliest man-made object found in Wales is an old stone age hand-axe made of quartzite discovered at Pen-y-lan, Cardiff, and estimated to be about 200,000 years old. Whereas old stone age man was first and foremost a hunter, new stone age man was more settled and gradually he developed the arts of agriculture and pottery making. The chief evidence of these later peoples is the massive communal tombs which they laboriously erected in the Vale of Glamorgan and the Gower peninsula.

During the bronze age which followed people were buried individually, usually after cremation. Hundreds of bronze age burial sites are known in all parts of Glamorgan, the most distinctive being those in the upland and moorland areas, where they are usually covered by distinctive stone cairns.

The iron age is associated with ironmaking, but the iron age people were also great builders. During this period, from about 800 BC to the first century AD, they constructed numerous promontory forts on coastal headlands and large hillforts inland protected by earthen ramparts.

The Roman occupation and the dark ages

It was not until about AD 75, more than three decades after their initial invasion of Britain, that the Roman armies marched into Glamorgan following the setting up of their legionary fortress at Caerleon in Gwent. The Romans constructed eight forts, including Cardiff and Neath, from which to exert their military authority. When conditions became more settled they built villas in the countryside, mainly in the Vale and Gower.

After the departure of the Romans there followed the long mysterious period known as the dark ages. Some of the hillforts continued to be occupied and a tenuous link was still maintained with Mediterranean lands. Christianity came early to this part of Britain and the rapid spread of Celtic monasticism in the late fifth century led to the establishment of monasteries at Llantwit Major, Llancarfan and Llandough near the coast. Through their missionaries, notably St Patrick, they helped to kindle the flame of Christianity in other parts of Wales and Ireland. Although none of the Celtic churches has survived, many early Christian crosses still stand as reminders of this enigmatic period.

It was during the dark ages that the political map of Wales was beginning to take shape. The bulk of Glamorgan, comprising the Vale and the *Blaenau*, formed the kingdom of Morgannwg. The land west of the Tawe river, known as Gwyr (the Welsh equivalent of Gower), belonged to the kingdom of Seisyllwg. For a few years in the middle of the eleventh century Morgannwg became politically united with Seisyllwg and the rest of Wales under the banner of Gruffydd ap Llywelyn.

The middle ages

Within a few years of Gruffydd's death the Normans arrived at the borders of Wales and from their newly established castle at Chepstow in Gwent they pushed on westwards through the Vale of Glamorgan, erecting timber castles as they went, firstly at Cardiff in about 1081 and then at Ogmore, Neath and Swansea; by 1116 they reached Loughor and built another castle there. The Welsh, refusing to capitulate, withdrew to the hills, and for two centuries the *Blaenau* was left in the hands of the Welsh rulers subject to the overlordship of the Anglo-Normans. It was an uneasy relationship, however, and in order to safeguard their newly won territory the invaders rebuilt their castles in stone and added further castles throughout the Vale and Gower. The end of any semblance of Welsh independence in Morgannwg came with the building of Caerphilly Castle in 1266

The marina at Swansea.

to counter the growing strength and threat of Llywelyn II, Prince of Wales. Although Llywelyn destroyed the unfinished castle in 1270 it was rebuilt on a massive scale and the Welsh prince was forced to retreat northwards.

Religion in Glamorgan

With the coming of the Normans the church was fundamentally reorganised. New stone-built churches were erected throughout the Vale and Gower and a system of dioceses, with Norman bishops, and parishes was introduced. Churches were also built in the upland areas but they were few in number and architecturally poorer. The Anglo-Norman lords also established monasteries – usually derived from mother churches in France – at Ewenny, Llangennith, Margam and Neath, and two friaries in Cardiff. Following Henry VIII's break with Rome in 1534 the monasteries were dissolved and their estates broken up. Ewenny and Margam became parish churches but the others fell into ruin or disappeared completely.

During the seventeenth century noncon-formity began to develop in Glamorgan. The first Baptist chapel was established in 1649 at Ilston in the Gower peninsula. In the eighteenth century a great religious awakening, resulting in the Methodist Revival, swept through Glamorgan and the rest of Wales. Methodism emphasised the emotional side of religion and it soon came to influence not only the religious life of Wales, but also its social and political life. Nowhere was this more so than in Glamorgan, which was then beginning a rapid industrial development. During the nineteenth century many hundreds of chapels were built in the newly industrialised areas and the coal-mining valleys became centres of religious and political nonconformity.

The industrial revolution

The depletion of timber sources for charcoal burning in southern England in the sixteenth century led Sussex ironmasters to move into Glamorgan about 1550 to set up new smelting centres amongst the hills, where, as

5

well as plentiful supplies of timber, there were also fast-running streams, to provide power, and iron ore and limestone. As coal took the place of charcoal and steam power replaced water power, the nature of the industry changed. The small scattered ironworks were replaced during the late eighteenth and early nineteenth centuries by vast new undertakings, employing thousands of workers, located around Merthyr Tydfil and in some of the valleys.

Meanwhile copper smelting had been started in the Vale of Neath at Aberdulais in 1584. Neath remained the chief centre of the industry until the eighteenth century, when it moved to the Swansea area because of the better harbour there. The success of copper smelting led to the establishment of other smelting industries, such as lead, silver, nickel and zinc, so that Swansea became known as the 'metallurgical capital of the world'.

At first coal was mined in the valleys mainly to serve the various metal industries. Then gradually, as its advantages became recognised, coal was mined more and more for general sale and this resulted in the sinking of hundreds of collieries right across Glamorgan.

The construction of the Taff Vale Railway in 1840/1 encouraged the export of coal from the valleys and led to Cardiff becoming the largest coal port in the world by 1914.

Glamorgan in the twentieth century

Much has changed during the twentieth century, particularly since the Second World War. Although steel is still made at Port Talbot the metallurgical industries generally and coal mining have undergone continuous decline. In the *Blaenau*, traditionally the most Welsh part of Glamorgan, the decline in heavy industries has been accompanied by a decline in the Welsh language to the extent that whereas fifty years ago more than a third of the population spoke Welsh now fewer than ten per cent are able to do so. While the upland areas have tended to decline the lowland areas have thrived. Cardiff and Swansea have continued to expand although the maritime trade on which they were based has decreased. Both are university cities and important shopping and cultural centres; both too have rejuvenated their dockland areas as a symbol of optimism for the future.

Craig y Llyn.

Three Cliffs Bay, Gower Area of Outstanding Natural Beauty.

2
Coast and countryside

Glamorgan, being a county situated between the sea and the mountains, is a region of contrasts. The coast becomes more rugged the further one goes west until it reaches the rocky cliffscape of the Gower peninsula, an Area of Outstanding Natural Beauty. The further north one travels, the higher and barer the hills become, until they merge with the mountains of the Brecon Beacons National Park, part of which extends into Glamorgan. In between these wilder areas are the softer landscapes of the Vale of Glamorgan and the 'Valleys', many of which are forested and greener now than they have been for many years. Information about waymarked walks in the numerous forests can be obtained from the visitor centres at Garwnant (telephone: 0685 723060) and Afan Argoed (telephone: 0639 850564).

This chapter describes some of the better known and more easily accessible landscape and natural history sites.

Aberdulais Waterfall, Aberdulais (OS 170: SS 772995). National Trust.

This fine waterfall, despite industrialisation, still storms into a rocky gorge. In the eighteenth and early nineteenth centuries it attracted many painters, including Turner. (For the visitor centre see chapter 8.)

Afan Argoed Country Park. Countryside visitor centre at Cynonville (OS 170: SS 820951). Telephone: 0639 850564. On A4107 between Port Talbot and Cymmer.

The 140 acre (56 ha) park includes a length of steep, forested hills with extensive views. A number of walks, varying from half a mile (800 metres) to 5 miles (8 km) in length, start from the centre, where there is also the Welsh Miners Museum (see chapter 7). It is possible to walk from Afan Argoed along the Coed Morgannwg long-distance forest walk north-eastwards to Craig y Llyn (SN 924031), near Hirwaun, or south to Margam Park (SS 813849).

Brecon Beacons National Park, just north of Merthyr Tydfil. Information from: National Park Office, Glamorgan Street, Brecon, Powys. Telephone: 0874 4437.

The small part of the National Park lying within the administrative county of Mid Glamorgan is all wild moorland rising to 1650 feet (503 metres), mostly consisting of limestone, with numerous swallow-holes, some rocky outcrops and some areas of afforestation.

There is a visitor centre in the Garwnant Forest (telephone: 0685 723060) at the upper end of Llwyn-on Reservoir (OS 160: SS 002131), where the emphasis is on forestry in relation to water supply, farming and the National Park. A circular forest walk, which can be divided into shorter walks depending on time available, starts from the centre. The full 3¹/₂ mile (5 km) circuit takes in a viewpoint formed from a limestone outcrop with good views of the Taf valley and the Brecon Beacons. South of the reservoir there is a Forest Nature Reserve at Pen-moel-allt on the west bank of the Afon Taf Fawr, while the wood below the Daren Fach limestone cliffs on the east bank is the home of *Sorbus leyana*, a rare species known only in this valley. Just beyond Pontsticill, at the car park (OS 160: SO 057119) near the Taf Fechan Reservoir dam, a 10 mile (15 km) waymarked walk leads through forestry land and eventually on to open moorland (in Powys) with grand views of the Brecon Beacons to the north.

Further west the headwaters of the Neath river divide into the Afon Mellte, Afon Nedd and Afon Pyrddin, all fast-flowing rivers which cascade down numerous waterfalls through deep, thickly wooded gorges. From the car park (OS 160: SN 911079) half a mile (800 metres) east of Pont-Nedd Fechan a winding footpath follows the Mellte eastwards for 2 miles (3 km) to the splendid Scwd-yr-Eira ('Spout of Snow') waterfall, where the rock has been so under-cut that it is possible to walk behind the water as it leaps downwards. The waterfalls on the Pyrddin can also be reached on foot from Pont-Nedd Fechan, but only by following the footpath on the Powys side of the river.

Bryngarw Country Park, Abergarw (OS 170: SS 904856). Telephone: warden, 0656 725155. Off A4065 north of Bridgend.

This delightful country park alongside the Afon Garw has a Japanese garden and riverside, woodland and meadow walks. Bryngarw House was originally a medieval farmhouse but was considerably enlarged and altered later.

Clyne Country Park, Swansea. See chapter 6.

Coed Morgannwg Way

This very attractive 27 mile (43 km) long-distance walk through forests, over mountains and across coalfield valleys is for the energetic. It starts at the Dare Valley Country Park (OS 170: SN 985025), near Aberdare, in the north, and ends at Margam Country Park (OS 170: SS 813849), near Port Talbot, in the south. 4 miles (6 km) from the start the walk passes Craig y Llyn (car park at OS 170: SN 924031), a cliff-faced peak (1969 feet; 600 metres) with expansive views across the Rhondda valleys and the moorlands of the Brecon Beacons. Coed Morgannwg, the largest forest in Glamorgan, covers about 40,000 acres (16,000 ha) and was largely planted during the Great Depression of the 1930s when many thousands of local miners were out of work.

Cosmeston Lakes Country Park, near Penarth (car park at OS 171: ST 179692). Telephone: warden, 0222 701678.

This 200 acre (83 ha) park is centred on two lakes which were originally limestone quarries divided by a lane. Surrounding the lakes there is a variety of landscapes with contrasting wildlife areas. The eastern lake is used for windsurfing, canoeing and sailing and has a children's playground nearby. (For the reconstructed medieval village in the park see chapter 3.)

Craig y Llyn hill walk, north of Treherbert (OS 170: SN 922025).

The 2¹/₂ mile (4 km) waymarked footpath starts from the Rhondda Visitor Centre (open August only), follows the ridge to the top of Craig y Llyn (1969 feet; 600 metres) and offers superb views across the upper end of the Vale of Neath towards the Brecon Beacons National Park.

Dare Valley Country Park. Visitor centre near Cwmdare (OS 170: SN 985025). Telephone: 0685 883099. Off B4277, via Highland Place from Aberdare.

The 483 acre (195 ha) park occupies most of the Dare valley from the outskirts of Aberdare to the craggy cliffs of Tarren y Bwllfa and the Berw-ddu waterfall near the source of the river. The valley was once full of collieries but all have been swept away. One at the upper end was used as the entrance to a complex of coal workings that had their exit in the Rhondda Fach valley. There are three small lakes and a man-made cascade which carries the

Cliffs at St Donat's, Glamorgan Heritage Coast.

river from the upper level down to the pre-mining level of the valley floor. A number of walks, varying from $2^{1}/_{2}$ to 4 miles (4 to 6 km) start at the visitor centre, which has been built with stone taken from redundant chapels in the area. The Coed Morgannwg Way long-distance footpath starts here.

Flat Holm. The island is accessible by boat (three or four sailings a week in summer) from Barry. Telephone: Flat Holm Project, 0446 747661.

Flat Holm lies in the middle of the Bristol Channel $4^{1}/_{2}$ miles (7 km) south-east of Penarth and was used as a refuge by Norsemen for their raids on the surrounding coasts during the tenth century. The island is roughly circular with an average diameter of 600 yards (550 metres) and, although flat and low-lying, has a rocky foreshore. The most striking ecological features of the island are its very active gull colony and its long-established, seemingly tame rabbit population. In 1972 the island was designated as a Site of Special Scientific Interest and the island's only farm is now used as a centre for the local nature reserve. In 1897 Marconi transmitted the first ever wireless message across water from Flat Holm to Lavernock Point near Penarth. (For the light-house and fortifications see chapter 8.)

Glamorgan Canal Nature Reserve, north of Cardiff (OS 171: ST 143804). Off Velindre Road, Whitchurch.

This is the last remaining water-filled stretch of the famous canal constructed in 1792-4 to link Merthyr Tydfil with Cardiff and provide a means of transporting iron from the furnaces to the port. It is rich in bird life and water plants. At the northern end a canal lock survives. (See also Three Castles Cycle Route, below.)

Glamorgan Heritage Coast, near South-erndown. Heritage centre at Dunraven Park (OS 170: SS 887732). Telephone: 0656 880157.

The Glamorgan Heritage Coast was desig-nated in 1972 and includes 14 miles (23 km) of coastline overlooking the Bristol Channel be-tween Aberthaw and Porthcawl. A clifftop walk runs from near the Aberthaw power station, passing a series of iron age promon-tory forts on the way, to Cwm Nash, near Monknash. The semicircular fort at Summer-house Point (see chapter 3) is unmistakable and easily accessible. Next to it is the **Seawatch Centre**, housed in a converted coastguard station, from where visitors can observe ships passing up and down the Bristol Channel. At **Nash Point** (car park at SS 917683) the lime-

Worms Head, Rhosili, Gower Area of Outstanding Natural Beauty.

stone rock strata of the cliffs are clearly exposed in textbook-like detail, with bare rock terraces forming the beach below. **Dunraven Park** (car park at SS 885730) has another promontory fort, a fine cliff walk and walled gardens with themed planting and an ice tower. **Merthyr Mawr Warren** at the western end (car park at SS 871772) is in complete contrast to the rest of the Heritage Coast, being covered in wind-blown sand. The sand rests on a limestone outcrop, making it the highest system of dunes in Britain. Many of the inland dunes are covered in vegetation, which has increased dramatically since myxomatosis devastated the rabbit population.

Gower Area of Outstanding Natural Beauty
The Gower peninsula was the first Area of Outstanding Natural Beauty to be designated in Britain. That was in 1956, to prevent this area of classic coastal scenery from being spoiled by undesirable development. All the following places, except Oxwich Burrows, belong to the National Trust, which owns about 5000 acres (2000 ha) of coastline, downs and saltmarsh on the peninsula.
Bishopston Valley, a long twisting valley with hanging woods, lies nearest to Swansea and leads down to a secluded beach at Pwll-du

Bay. Beyond are 3 miles (5 km) of limestone cliffs between Pwll-du Bay and Three Cliffs Bay. There is a car park at Southgate (OS 159: SS 554875) from which footpaths follow the clifftops. The cliffs are honeycombed with small caves and occasional larger ones, such as Bacon Hole and Michin Hole, which are accessible only at low tide. **Three Cliffs Bay** gets its name from three jagged limestone cliffs which project from the mainland and protect its sandy beach. At **Oxwich Burrows** (car park at SS 501864) there is a wide curving beach, with a mile-long (1.6 km) sand trail, backed by wind-blown sand dunes which have blocked off the river to form an extensive marsh with several freshwater pools. It is a National Nature Reserve with a wide range of plants, wildfowl and waders.
From Port Eynon (car park at SS 467851), with its curious dovecote in a walled-up cave at Culver Hole, there is a splendid 6 mile (9 km) clifftop walk to Rhosili. **Rhosili** (car park at SS 415880) stands high above the coast and the only way down to the superb 3 mile (5 km) long beach is on foot. A clifftop walk leads to the furthest tip of Gower, an island known evocatively as Worms Head ('worm' meaning dragon). The island is another National Nature Reserve, notable for its plant and bird life

and accessible only at low tide. There is a National Trust visitor centre at Rhosili with displays relating to Gower's history, landscape and wildlife.

The northern coast of the Gower peninsula is less popular with visitors than the southern coast but its more reticent scenery, including a fine line of inland cliffs near Landimore, is well worth exploring. **Whitford Burrows** is a National Nature Reserve (information kiosk near Cwm Ivy, SS 437940). It has great outcrops of limestone, forests of ash and Corsican pine, an avenue of Monterey pine and a 2 mile (3 km) long spit of massive lime-rich sand dunes, with a number of damp hollows or slacks, backing on to widespread saltmarshes. At Whitford Point, standing just above the low-water mark, is an unusual cast iron lighthouse, long unmanned, which was built in 1865.

Gower Farm Trail and Farm Museum, Lake Farm, Llanddewi, near Knelston. (OS 159: SS 461892). Telephone: 0792 391195.

The two waymarked farm trails start at the Farm Museum car park, pass Llanddewi church (see chapter 5) and then follow green lanes and farm tracks across fields. The longer trail (6 miles; 9 km) passes Harding's Down with its hillforts (see chapter 3). The farm museum has been converted from a farmhouse and contains displays of farm machinery and domestic artefacts as well as having farmyard animals and birds.

Hensol Forest, Welsh St Donats (OS 170: ST 041763).

This is a scattered forest with a delightful lake, Llyn Pysgodlyn, and two picnic places, at ST 038764 and ST 033768, with waymarked walks within easy reach of Cardiff.

Kenfig Burrows, near Kenfig (OS 170: SS 803812).

This nature reserve comprises extensive sand dunes, a freshwater lake and marshes and provides many walks around Kenfig Pool and along the sea shore. North of Kenfig Pool there was, in the fourteenth century, a substantial and flourishing borough. The town was gradually overwhelmed by the sand in the fifteenth century and all that can be seen now are a few broken walls belonging to Kenfig Castle (SS 801827) rising above the dunes (see chapter 4).

Gower Farm Museum, Llanddewi.

11

Parc Cwm Darran, north of Bargoed (OS 171: SO 119031). On secondary road between Deri and Fochriw.

This small country park is on land reclaimed from colliery workings along the bottom of the valley. It includes two small reservoirs, woodland and heathland.

Penscynor Wildlife Park, Cilfrew. See chapter 9.

Porthkerry Country Park, Park Road, Barry (OS 171: ST 099672).

This pleasant valley with woodlands and meadows leading down to a storm-washed pebble beach is situated on the western edge of the town. There are massive cliffs at the seaward end of the park, and nature trails, picnic sites, a children's playground and mini-golf course inland.

Ridgeway Walk (Ffordd y Bryniau)

This 21 mile (32 km), mainly moorland walk starts on Mynydd y Gaer (OS 170: SS 969859), north-east of Bridgend, and finishes on Caerphilly Common (OS 171: ST 156853). The walk varies from ancient upland tracks and forest trails to urban footpaths and includes a visit to the hill town of Llantrisant with its cobbled lanes. There are extensive views of the mining valleys to the north and the coastal plain to the south from many points along the way. The highest point (1007 feet; 307 metres) is reached on Garth Hill (OS 171: ST 103835), with its bronze age burial mounds overlooking the Taff Gorge.

Sully Island. Car park at Swanbridge, off B4267 between Barry and Penarth (OS 171: ST 166674).

This small low elongated island is attached to the mainland by a rocky causeway and accessible on foot at low tide. There are remains of an iron age promontory fort at the eastern end. A hoard of Roman coins was unearthed here in 1899.

Three Castles Cycle Route: North Road, Cardiff (OS 171: ST 179771) to Castell Coch (OS 171: ST 131826).

This 6 mile (10 km) cycle track starts at the Welsh College of Music and Drama, just to the north of Cardiff Castle, and runs through Bute Park, Cardiff's 'green lung'. It then follows the Afon Taf through Llandaff North and Whitchurch, past the Glamorgan Canal Nature Reserve and then on to the village of Tongwynlais, where the road and lane can be followed up to the exotic Castell Coch (see chapter 6). For the more energetic the track can be continued for a further 5 miles (8 km) of hilly country towards Caerphilly Castle.

Cilifor Top hillfort, Llanrhidian.

Reconstructed north gate of Roman fort, Cardiff Castle.

3
Places of archaeological interest

Glamorgan has many archaeological sites ranging from palaeolithic (old stone age) cave settlements to lost medieval villages, and including neolithic (new stone age) burial chambers, bronze age cairn circles, iron age forts, Roman forts and an early Christian settlement. Early Christian crosses which survive at Llandough, Llantwit Major and Margam are included in chapter 5. Many artefacts, such as stone tools, funerary beakers, coins and weapons from archaeological sites can be seen in local museums and especially at the National Museum of Wales in Cardiff.

In the following gazetteer the relevant Ordnance Survey 1:50,000 map sheet number and the National Grid reference are given for each archaeological site.

The Bulwark, Llanmadoc (OS 159: SS 443927). National Trust.

This is a large oval iron age hillfort at the eastern end of Llanmadoc Hill. It was probably built with a single embankment but modified later with multiple earthen ramparts, closely spaced at the western end but more widely spaced near the entrance on the east side. To the west of the hillfort are the remains of fourteen bronze age round cairns, all of which have been severely robbed. In 1867, when first recorded, there were nineteen cairns.

Burry Holms, on the coast west of Llangennith (OS 159: SS 400926).

There are remains of an iron age promontory fort and an early Christian settlement on this small limestone island at the north-western tip of the Gower peninsula. A rocky causeway connects the island to the mainland except at high tide. The fort lies at the western end of the island and is protected by a bank and ditch running across the width of the island. The early Christian settlement lies on the sheltered eastern side. Excavations carried out between 1965 and 1969 revealed a small early twelfth-century stone church with an apsidal east end partly surrounded by an oval enclosure wall, twelfth-century dwellings, a thirteenth or fourteenth-century hall-house and a late medieval school or meeting room. Below the walls of the church were found corner post-holes belonging to an earlier, and even tinier, timber church 12 feet (3.7 metres) long by 11 feet (3.3 metres) wide; this was possibly the church of Caradog, who was in this area in 1089.

Caerau hillfort, Ely, Cardiff (OS 171: ST 133750).

This very large triangular iron age hillfort was fortified with triple embankments on the north and south sides but only by a single massive rampart and ditch (broken by an inturned entrance) on the eastern side. Pre-Roman and Romano-British pottery has been discovered on the site. Within the north-eastern corner of the hillfort there is an oval embankment belonging to a medieval ring-work castle. The small thirteenth-century church with a saddleback tower standing next to the ringwork possibly indicates that there was once a village here.

Cardiff Roman fort, Cardiff Castle, Cardiff (OS 171: ST 181766).

The curtain walls of the medieval castle are built, on two and a half sides, over the remains of a quadrangular Roman fort. The fort was erected in the late third or early fourth century AD as a defence against sea raiders and to replace several earlier forts. A long stretch of the Roman masonry walls, with remains of five-sided towers, can be seen in a gallery constructed below the earthen banks behind the curtain walls. The curtain walls were restored in realistic imitation of the Roman originals, although higher, by Lord Bute in the late nineteenth century.

Carn Bugail burial chamber, near Bedlinog (OS 171: SO 100035).

On the summit of Gelligaer Common, 4 miles (6 km) north of Gelligaer, there are the remains of a large circular mound with a central grave. The oval capstone of this bronze age burial chamber has been slightly displaced. Further north are remains of another, much smaller burial chamber. The 'inscribed stone' shown on the Ordnance Survey map to the south-east is early Christian in date but has now lost its inscription.

Carn Llechart burial chamber and cairn circle, near Pontardawe (OS 160: SN 697063).

The neolithic burial chamber has been much disturbed and now consists of a collection of stone slabs and some small uprights. Nearby, at the side of the trackway, is one of the best preserved bronze age burial sites in Glamorgan, comprising a circle of 25 contiguous slabs around a central grave. 600 yards (550 metres) to the north-west is a cairn cemetery of sixteen small cairns distributed on both sides of the trackway.

Cilifor Top hillfort, near Llanrhidian (OS 159: SS 505923).

This is a large hillfort, 7½ acres (3 ha) in extent, with ramparts following the contours of the hill. On the steep north-eastern slope a

Main street at Cosmeston medieval village.

single rampart suffices; the multiple ramparts elsewhere were probably added later. The entrance to the enclosure is at the south-west and its present zigzag approach may be the result of later alterations. There are indications of several hut platforms in the interior of the hillfort at the northern end.

Cosmeston medieval village, Cosmeston Lakes Country Park, near Penarth (OS 171: ST 177689). Telephone: 0222 708686.

Cosmeston was once a sizeable village but the Black Death and poor economic conditions during the fourteenth century probably led to its becoming deserted. By 1437 the manor house itself was in ruins. The site of the 'lost' village has been gradually excavated since 1982. Fourteenth-century houses, farm buildings and a circular dovecote have been unearthed. Following excavation, each building is being reconstructed using traditional methods of construction. The reconstructed buildings include a farmstead, a barn and a kiln house lying alongside the former village street. Interesting experiments with medieval crops have also been undertaken.

Dunraven promontory fort, St Bride's Major (OS 170: SS 887726).

The iron age fort occupies a rocky peninsula known as Trwyn-y-witch, near Southerndown. Along the steeply sloping northern side of the ridge the defenders built double ramparts. Sea erosion has destroyed the original entrance on the west side and has reduced the fort from about 25 acres (10 ha) to 16 acres (6.5 ha) in area. Hollows and ledges on the northern slope of the headland may be the sites of iron age dwellings while three long pillow mounds across the point of the peninsula are the sites of medieval rabbit warrens.

Glan-y-Mor Roman site, The Knap, Barry (OS 171: ST 099664).

This Roman domestic building was excavated in 1980-1 and saved from development. The remains comprise footings of walls belonging to a series of rooms arranged around a central courtyard. The building was probably built in the late third or early fourth century AD but its function has eluded discovery.

Hardings Down hillforts, Llangennith (OS 159: SS 434907).

A group of iron age defended enclosures occupies rather weak sites on the down just south of the village. The most substantial enclosure is the West Camp, which is oval in plan and is defended by a bank, ditch and counterscarp; there are remains of two further ramparts on the south-eastern side. Excavations in 1962 revealed a gateway at the north-east end and remains of two circular huts in the interior. The East Camp crowned the summit but appears never to have been completed. A third, much smaller enclosure is sited on the steeper northern slopes.

Maen Ceti (Arthur's Stone) burial chamber, north-east of Reynoldston (OS 159: SS 491905).

This unusual burial chamber on the slopes of Cefn Bryn appears to have been formed by hollowing out the ground under an enormous glacial boulder. The boulder was underpinned by ten upright stones to form two irregularly shaped burial compartments. There is no evidence that the cromlech was ever covered by the usual mound. The monument's alternative name is derived from a legend that Arthur found a pebble in his shoe while out walking near Llanelli and threw it across the water to land on the Gower peninsula.

Maes-y-felin burial chamber, west of St Lythans (OS 171: ST 101723). Cadw.

The burial chamber stands in skeletal form in an open field. Three large rugged slabs support a massive capstone to form a rectangular chamber. It is not certain if the chamber was ever covered by a mound.

Nash promontory fort, near Marcross (OS 170: SS 915683).

Although erosion by the sea has reduced the interior of this iron age fort to a narrow, flat-topped ridge the defensive nature of the layout is still clear. The steep eastern side overlooks a narrow valley and is defended by a bank which turns in towards the entrance at the northern end, where four parallel banks further strengthened the fort.

Neath Roman fort (Nidum), Dwr-y-felin, Neath (OS 170: SS 748976).

Fragmentary remains of the fort can be seen in the housing estate near Neath Abbey Road. They include the masonry foundations of the south-west and south-east gates and part of a ditch. The fort was originally erected in earth and timber about AD 75 and rebuilt in stone in 120.

Maes-y-felin burial chamber.

Parc Le Breos burial chamber, near Parkmill (OS 159: SS 537898). Cadw.

This is a good example of a neolithic multi-chambered tomb and exhibits most of the classic features of the type known as Severn-Cotswold. The tomb was constructed about 4000-3500 BC. It is wedge-shaped and built of thin slabs of dry stone. A bell-shaped forecourt leads to a central passage, off which are four small side chambers. Nearby, on the steep side of a wooded valley (at SS 538900), is the **Cat Hole** cave dwelling. The cave, which

has two entrances, was occupied in both the palaeolithic and the mesolithic periods; during the bronze age it was used for burial while in the medieval period it was reused as a dwelling.

Paviland Caves, near Port Eynon (OS 159: SS 437860). National Trust.

Situated amongst the cliffs 2 miles (3 km) west of Port Eynon are two caves known as **Goat's Hole** and **Hound's Hole**, which can be reached from the sands at low tide. They are not easy to get to, however, and the unwary can be cut off by high tides; nevertheless, they are included here because of their importance to British prehistory and the history of British archaeology. In 1823 Dean Buckland discovered a headless skeleton in the 70 foot (22 metre) long Goat's Hole. It lay among the bones of ice age mammals, including mammoth, bear and woolly rhinoceros. Because of its covering of red iron-oxide deposits it became famous as the 'Red Lady of Paviland', but in fact it was the skeleton of a young man who lived during the old stone age more than twenty thousand years ago, at a time when the caves looked out across a wooded plain rather than the sea. The **Longhole Cave**, 1 mile (1.6 km) west of Port Eynon, is near the top of the cliffs and is easier to reach. It was excavated in 1861 and was one of the earliest examples in

Nash promontory fort, near Marcross: aerial view.

Tinkinswood burial chamber.

which the contemporary association of flint artefacts with extinct animal remains was indisputably proved.

Pwll-du promontory fort, Pennard (OS 159: SS 568866). National Trust.

Situated over 200 feet (75 metres) above the sea on a cliff headland, this iron age fort was defended on the landward side by two widely spaced lines of ramparts and a ditch interspersed with rocky outcrops. Excavation has revealed the sites of a timber gateway and three huts and has shown that the fort was still occupied in the Roman period.

Sully Island promontory fort. See chapter 2.

Summerhouse Camp promontory fort, near Llantwit Major (OS 170: SS 994665).

The fort is now, as a result of cliff erosion, semicircular in plan and occupies a spur of land between a valley and cliffs overlooking the sea. The outer defences comprise two large ramparts with accompanying ditches. The entrance was probably on the eastern side. At the heart of the complex there is a smaller, and possibly earlier, enclosure defended by a bank and ditch. An octagonal summerhouse was built during the eighteenth century on the west side between the outer and inner defences.

Thurba Head and The Knave promontory forts, Rhosili (OS 159: SS 422871 and SS 432864). National Trust.

Thurba Head fort is comparatively small and is located on a rocky spur 1 mile (1.6 km) south-east of Rhosili. It appears to have been built in two phases: an earlier part defended by a curving stone wall, and a later part defended by two banks and ditches across the neck of the promontory. There are remains of five hut circles within the fort. The Knave fort is another small 'cliff-castle' a mile (1.6 km) further east. It is defended by two widely spaced limestone ramparts and ditches.

Tinkinswood burial chamber, St Nicholas (OS 171: ST 092733). Cadw.

This neolithic burial chamber was the first of its kind to be excavated in a comparatively scientific way, in 1914. The mound is almost rectangular and is held in place by a dry stone wall. The main chamber is entered from a recessed forecourt at the east end and is covered by an enormous capstone, which, at an estimated 50 tons weight, is the largest in Britain. The excavation revealed the remains of at least fifty people in the main chamber.

Warren medieval settlement, Rhosili (OS 159: SS 416883).

The remains of a sand-engulfed village and church of the twelfth and thirteenth centuries are located immediately north of Rhosili on the Burrows above the beach. They were partly excavated in 1980. Narrow strip fields, known locally as **The Viel**, have survived from the medieval period on the headland between the present village and Worms Head.

Caerphilly Castle.

4
Castles and monastic ruins

Glamorgan is a land of castles. At one time there were some forty stone castles within the county – more than for the whole of northern Wales. Fourteen of these castles are open to the public or are freely accessible, while others can be easily seen from outside. Most were built by the Anglo-Normans or by their successors to defend their newly won territories and are situated in the southern and western parts of the county. Very few stone castles were built in Glamorgan by the Welsh nobility.

The Normans also founded several monastic houses in the areas they occupied, chiefly in the Vale of Glamorgan. The monasteries, like the castles, have had mixed histories: some have disappeared completely; some have survived only as picturesque ruins, while others were adapted to meet the needs of the times and became parish churches.

Bishop's Castle, High Street, Llandaf, Cardiff (OS 171: ST 156779).

This small castle has long been associated with the Bishops of Llandaf but it may have been built by Gilbert de Clare, the powerful lord of Cardiff, in the late thirteenth century when the see was temporarily vacant. A massive twin-towered gatehouse faces the street and leads into a roughly quadrangular courtyard enclosed by high curtain walls with small towers at the corners. Remains of two large windows at the north-eastern corner indicate the site of the great hall. According to tradition, the castle was burnt by Owain Glyndwr in 1404 during his war of independence, after which the Bishop of Llandaf moved to more comfortable and safer quarters at Mathern in Gwent.

Caerphilly Castle, Caerphilly (OS 171: ST 156871). Telephone: 0222 883143. Cadw.

Caerphilly Castle covers an area of 30 acres (12 ha), making it the largest castle in Wales. It was built not by a king, as its majestic scale would suggest, but by a Norman baron, Gilbert de Clare, as a formidable redoubt to withstand the threats of Llywelyn ap Gruffudd, Prince of

18

Wales. Work on the castle began in 1268 and was interrupted in 1270 when Llywelyn set fire to it. De Clare recommended building in 1271 and construction continued into the early fourteenth century. From the air the castle appears to be on an island surrounded by water, although it comprises a concentric citadel with inner and outer curtain walls surrounded by an inner moat, which, in turn, is defended by two artificial lakes, a mighty stone barrage wall, which also serves as a fortified fighting platform, and an outer moat. The citadel, or inner ward, is quadrangular in plan with round towers at the corners and massive twin-towered gatehouses at the entrances. The great hall on the south side of the inner ward is a generously proportioned room with elaborately decorated windows on the north side (added in the early fourteenth century by Hugh le Despenser). The great hall was served by vast kitchens on the south side of the inner-ward curtain wall and has a cross-passage leading down to a watergate on the south lake. One of the corner towers of the inner ward leans 11 feet (3.3 metres) out of the perpendicular at an angle comparable to that of the Leaning Tower of Pisa. The inner ward is surrounded by a narrow middle ward, with its own low curtain walls and gatehouses, and then by the south lake and the inner moat. To the west there is an outer bailey in the form of an island between the inner moat and the northern and southern lakes. To the east are the northern and southern platforms, each with its own gatehouse at the extremities of the platforms, built on the stone barrage with another twin-towered gatehouse in the centre forming the main entrance to the site and connected to the middle ward and the land beyond the outer moat by modern drawbridges. Caerphilly Castle was the first truly concentric castle to be built in Britain and no other castle in the country has such a complex system of defence and counter-defence. In 1316 Llywelyn Bren of Senghenydd besieged the castle for more than a month and took the Sheriff of Glamorgan prisoner; but the uprising was short-lived and Llywelyn himself was taken prisoner in March and sent to the Tower of London. Considerable parts of the castle, notably two of the inner-ward towers, the east gatehouse of the inner ward and the great hall roof, were restored by the third and fourth Marquesses of Bute between 1868 and 1939.

Cardiff Castle, the Norman motte.

Candleston Castle, Merthyr Mawr (OS 170: SS 871772). Always open.

Fragmentary ruins of Candleston Castle rise out of the sand dunes near the car park at the end of the lane from Merthyr Mawr. It is not a true castle but a fortified manor house and the ruins comprise a fourteenth-century square tower with a later hall block. It was formerly owned by the Cantelupe family and by the Herbert family of Swansea and was still inhabited at the beginning of the nineteenth century.

Cardiff Castle, Cardiff (OS 171: ST 181766). Telephone: 0222 822083.

After the overthrow, about 1081, of Iestyn ap Gwrgan, the Welsh prince of Morgannwg, the Norman baron Fitzhamon took over the Roman fort (see chapter 3) and within its derelict walls raised an enormous mound, or motte, and built a timber stockade on top of it. This was an insufficient defence against the Welsh for in 1158 Ifor ap Meurig, the lord of Senghenydd, attacked the castle at night and, in the words of Gerald of Wales, 'secretly scaled the walls and seizing the count and countess with their only son, carried them off into the woods and did not release them until he had recovered everything that had been unjustly taken from him'. A short while later the Normans rebuilt the castle keep in stone and this splendid twelve-sided 'shell' keep, a perfect example of its type, still stands on top of the steep-sided mound surrounded by a wide water-filled moat. In the thirteenth century Gilbert de Clare added a new gatehouse to the keep and built the Black Tower on the site of the Roman south gate and strengthened the walls and gates of the castle.

The great hall and Octagon Tower in the west wing date from the mid fifteenth century and replaced the Keep Tower after more peaceful conditions had been brought about. In the eighteenth and nineteenth centuries, however, the west wing underwent radical alterations as improvements were made to turn the castle into a luxurious mansion. In 1777 Henry Holland restored the central block and added extensions at either end in the same style as the original Tudor wing for the first

Cardiff Castle, the west wing.

Marquess of Bute. In the late nineteenth century the third Marquess of Bute engaged William Burges, an architect of extraordinary imagination and wit, to 'restore' the castle. To the Octagonal Tower Burges added a marvellous spiky flèche, or spire, in 1872-5 and to the sixteenth-century Herbert Tower he added a steeply pitched roof with tall chimneys; the Bute Tower north of these was started in 1873 and as the *pièce de résistance* Burges added a tall clock-tower at the south-west corner. Inside the new and reconstructed towers Burges created fantastically rich interiors such as the Arab Room, reputedly copied from an Arabian harem, the Chaucer Room with exotic decoration to illustrate the author's writings, the Guest Room with walls inlaid with minerals and precious stones, and the Summer Smoking Room with its domed ceiling lined with mirrors. On the top of the Bute Tower there is a roof garden with a sunken courtyard containing a fountain surrounded by a cast iron arcade. An impressive military tattoo is held at Cardiff Castle every two years.

Castell Coch, Tongwynlais. See chapter 6.

Coity Castle, Coity (OS 170: SS 923815). Telephone: 0656 652021. Cadw.
Coity Castle is the largest and most splendid of three castles built near Bridgend to form a defensive triangle guarding the Ogwr valley. It is reputed to have been acquired by Payn de Turbeville, a Norman Marcher lord, from Morgan, the Welsh ruler of the district, in return for marrying Morgan's daughter Sybil. Gilbert de Turbeville replaced the original timber palisade around the circular inner ward in the late twelfth century with a stone curtain wall and erected a powerful square keep. In the thirteenth century a projecting round tower, three storeys high, was added on the southern side overlooking the moat, to provide defence from a flanking attack. The increasing wealth and influence of the Turbevilles in the fourteenth century resulted in extensive remodelling of the castle and additional new building. The outer ward was enclosed for the first time by a stone curtain wall with three projecting rectangular towers, and a strong middle gatehouse was constructed next to the keep to control access between the outer and inner wards. The keep itself was also improved and a chapel and a fine hall block with service rooms were built along the southern side of the inner ward.

In 1404 the castle was besieged by Owain Glyndwr and Parliament had to petition the king to send a relief force in November. A further relief force was despatched in September 1405 but its baggage train was plundered on the way. Meanwhile Glyndwr and his forces breached a large section of the north curtain wall of the inner ward.

Dinas Powys Castle, Dinas Powys (OS 171: ST 153716). Always open.
This castle stands on a ridge just behind the town and consists of a high stone curtain wall, probably dating from the fourteenth century, surrounding a large rectangular courtyard with remnants of a twelfth-century square keep tower at one end.

Ewenny Priory, Ewenny. See chapter 5.

Kenfig Castle, Kenfig (OS 170: SS 801827). Always open.
There are scant remains of the once strong, rectangular keep tower of Kenfig Castle surrounded by a wilderness of overgrown sand dunes. The keep was probably built in the twelfth century on a low motte and enclosed later by a bailey wall. The large bailey became the site of a substantial town with a church, all now lost under the sand dunes. The inundation appears to have started gradually, although already by the fourteenth century the advancing sands were troublesome enough for warnings to be issued against any act likely to make encroachment easier. In the early sixteenth century a sandstorm completed the process so that by 1540 Leland was able to observe that the town was 'in ruins and almost shokid an devourid with the sandes that the Severn Se ther castith up'. Kenfig continued to send a member to Parliament until the borough and corporation were abolished in 1883.

Loughor Castle, Loughor (OS 159: SS 564980). Cadw. Always open.
All that is left of Loughor Castle is a late thirteenth-century tower built on a natural spur overlooking the Llwchwr river and some traces of the curtain wall beneath the turf. The site was first used by the Romans, who built an auxiliary fort here about AD 75 to control the mouth of the river. By 1116 the Normans had arrived and they erected a ringwork castle of earth and timber on the spur of ground at the south-eastern corner of the Roman fort.

Margam Abbey, Margam. See chapter 5.

Morlais Castle, 2 miles (3 km) north of Merthyr Tydfil (OS 160: SO 048097). Always open.

The remains of Morlais Castle stand dramatically above the Taf Fechan Gorge on the northern rim of Glamorgan. The castle was built in the late thirteenth century on the site of an iron age hillfort by Gilbert de Clare, lord of Glamorgan, to guard the mountain route from Brecon into his domain. The west curtain wall is perched precariously at the edge of precipitous cliffs while the other sides are protected by an impressive rock-cut dry moat. All that remains of the circular keep is a half-buried lower room with a vaulted ceiling carried on a central column. There were four other round towers but only their bases remain above ground. In 1290-1 the castle became the centre of a legal dispute between de Clare and Humphrey de Bohun, lord of Brecon, which led to Edward I marching from northern Wales to Morlais to deal with his tiresome earls and then fining each heavily.

Neath Abbey, Neath (OS 170: SS 737974). Telephone: 0792 812387. Cadw.

The extensive ruins of Neath Abbey, blackened by a century and a half of industrial pollution, lie a mile (1.6 km) west of Neath near an industrial estate and between a canal and a railway. The abbey was founded in 1130 by Richard de Granville as a daughter house of the French abbey of Savigny, but in 1147 it became Cistercian when the Savigniacs were absorbed into that monastic order. The original building soon became too small for the growing community and the buildings which can be seen today are mostly from the period when the abbey was rebuilt in the late twelfth and thirteenth centuries. The rather austere west range was erected between 1170 and 1220 for the lay brothers and is the oldest surviving part of the abbey. The chapter house and the dormitory range on the east side of the cloister all date from the mid thirteenth century. The five-bay undercroft beneath the dormitory still retains a fine rib-vaulted ceiling. The dormitory is linked to the monks' reredorter, or latrine block, on the east side by a bridge at first-floor level. In the late fifteenth century

Neath Abbey, the undercroft.

Ogmore Castle and stepping stones.

part of the dormitory and its undercroft were revamped and extended to create a house for the abbot. The great abbey church on the north side of the cloister was rebuilt between 1280 and 1330 on an ambitious scale with elaborate columns and decorated tile flooring. The medieval floor tiles which survived from the church have been taken up to prevent deterioration and are exhibited in the dormitory undercroft.

In the sixteenth century Neath Abbey was, according to Leland, 'the fairest abbay of all Wales'. George Borrow, writing three centuries later, described it as 'looking darkly grey, a ruin of vast size with window holes, towers, spires, and arches ... surrounded by grimy diabolical-looking buildings, in the neighbourhood of which were huge heaps of cinders and black rubbish'. Amongst the ruins are the remains of a Tudor mansion with a first-floor hall, which was built, after the dissolution of the monastery in 1539, over the dormitory undercroft and incorporated the later abbot's house.

Neath Castle, Neath (OS 170: SS 753978). Viewing of ruins from exterior only.

The existing Neath Castle, near the town centre, although completely rebuilt in stone in the thirteenth century, appears to be of twelfth-century origin. The compactly planned castle was built to a D-shaped layout with a strong twin-towered gateway, fronted by a barbican, on the west side and a massive half-round tower on the opposite side. The land falls very steeply on the west side, suggesting that at the time of the castle's construction the Nedd, or Neath, river flowed close by. The castle was captured by Llywelyn the Great in 1231 and in 1321 it was taken by the Marchers.

Newcastle Castle, Bridgend (OS 170: SS 902801). Telephone: 0656 652964. Cadw.

The castle stands on the edge of a steep scarp overlooking the Ogwr river and the town of Bridgend. The earliest castle on the site, probably an earth and timber ringwork, was built by Robert Fitzhamon in about 1100. It was reconstructed in stone in the late twelfth century as a single polygonal enclosure surrounded by a high curtain wall. The splendid main gateway is constructed to an unusually high quality and comprises a semicircular arch carried on columns with decorated capitals and ornamented with panel and pellet moulding. It may have been the work of royal masons during the period (1183-9) when the castle was held in ward by Henry II. The remains of two small square towers, one next to the gate and the other on the west side, straddle the curtain wall.

Ogmore Castle, Ogmore (OS 170: SS 882769). Telephone: 0656 653435. Cadw.

Ogmore Castle was erected close to the Ewenny by William de Londres about 1116

Porth Melin, Cowbridge.

to guard the important river crossing (still marked by stepping stones). Although very ruined, it still looks picturesque in its rural riverside setting. The castle is approached through the outer ward, which was defended by an earthen bank. Within the outer ward are the remains of the Court House, built, probably in the fourteenth century, to house the manorial court of the Dukes of Lancaster. The main surviving features of the castle itself are the early twelfth-century rectangular keep tower commanding the inner gate and the remains of a thirteenth-century hall tucked into the corner of the inner ward. The oval inner ward is defended by a rather weak curtain wall and by a wide moat on three sides, the fourth side being protected by the river. A replica of an eleventh-century cross slab (the original is in the National Museum of Wales at Cardiff) in the inner ward refers to the grant of land in the area to a local church long before the coming of the Normans.

Oxwich Castle, Oxwich. See chapter 6.

Oystermouth Castle, Swansea (OS 159: SS 613884).

The castle is in a park on a hill overlooking the sea. It is the largest of the Gower castles and occupies the site of an earlier fortification. The castle has a very irregular layout. The earliest part is the large rectangular keep tower which was built in the mid thirteenth century by the de Braose family. In 1287 the castle was severely damaged during the rebellion of Rhys ap Maredudd, but within a few years curtain

walls and a gateway were added and the keep was repaired and raised in height. The two circular towers which originally flanked the gateway have mostly gone. In the fourteenth century a new wing was added to the east of the keep. This contained the chapel, with its traceried windows, on the first floor.

Penlle'r Castell, north of Clydach (OS 159: SN 665096). Always open.

The remains of this fortification lie on the bare moorlands overlooking the Amman valley 6 miles (9 km) north of Clydach. The remains comprise a roughly rectangular mound divided into two unequal parts, all surrounded by a bank and a deep ditch. There are traces of a square tower on the smaller part of the mound and some dry stone huts on the larger part. The structure appears to have been erected during the late thirteenth century, possibly as a temporary strongpoint during a dispute between the Anglo-Norman lord of Gower, William de Braose, and Rhys Fychan.

Pennard Castle, Pennard (OS 159: SS 544855). Always open.

Only the twin-towered entrance gateway, the north curtain wall and a curious square building at the north-west angle have survived. The gateway and curtain wall were built during the late thirteenth century. The courtyard is now engulfed by sand but excavations in 1961 revealed the foundations of the hall on the west side of the ward. The ruins lie between a golf course and a deep valley and overlook Three Cliffs Bay.

Porth Melin and town wall, Cowbridge (OS 170: SS 994746).

The town wall was roughly oblong in plan with at least three gates, possibly four. The west gate was demolished in 1754 and the east gate about twenty years later. Only Porth Melin, the south gate, dating from about 1300 now survives. Part of the town wall and a circular corner tower west of Porth Melin also survive.

St Donat's Castle, St Donat's. See chapter 6.

St Fagans Castle, St Fagans. See chapter 6.

Swansea Castle, Swansea (OS 159: SS 657931). Cadw. Viewing from exterior only.

There was a Norman motte and bailey castle in Swansea from the beginning of the twelfth century. This was reconstructed in stone during the early thirteenth century, but when the buildings which survive today were erected it became known as the 'old castle'. The 'new castle' was built about 1300 just to the south of the original castle in a new outer ward. The remains comprise a square north tower and a southern block, joined by remnants of the curtain wall. The southern block has vaulted undercrofts at ground-floor level and a spacious hall and solar on the first floor. On the outer side it is crowned by a parapet with an eye-catching arcade of linked arches added in the

fourteenth century, possibly by Henry de Gower, Bishop of St Davids. The arcaded parapet is similar to those added by the same bishop to his palaces at St Davids and Lamphey. The north tower remained in use as a debtors' prison until 1858, when it was closed following a scandal concerning the neglect of its inmates.

Weobley Castle, Llanrhidian (OS 159: SS 478927). Telephone: 0792 390012. Cadw.

Weobley Castle is more of a fortified manor house than a castle, although its striking setting on the northern edge of the Gower plateau has a militaristic aspect. A simple gatehouse leads into an irregularly shaped courtyard around which are ranged mainly domestic buildings. The thick-walled tower, possibly dating from the mid thirteenth century, on the south side of the gatehouse is probably the oldest part of the 'castle'. The hall block on the northern side was erected in the late thirteenth century and the tower containing the lord's solar (with an exhibition and approached by modern timber stairs) between the gatehouse and the hall was added in the fourteenth century. During the Glyndwr rebellion, in 1409, Weobley Castle was badly damaged. Later in the fifteenth century the property passed to Sir Rhys ap Thomas, who added a two-storey porch to the northern range to give the hall and private rooms a more dignified entrance.

Swansea Castle, the parapet.

Beulah Chapel, Port Talbot.

5
Churches and chapels

Glamorgan was an early centre of Christianity in Britain and although nothing now remains of the buildings of the Celtic monastic centres, which were probably constructed in timber, the distribution of many inscribed stones and early Christian crosses in the coastal strip provides evidence of their influence (see Ewenny Priory, Llandaf Cathedral, Llandough, Llanmadoc, Llantrisant, Llantwit Major and Margam Stones Museum). In Llandaf Cathedral the county also has one of the oldest cathedrals in Britain. From the seventeenth century onwards nonconformity flourished in Glamorgan and while many nineteenth-century nonconformist chapels have been converted to other uses or pulled down to make way for development there are still many worth looking at. The nineteenth century also left a rich heritage of Anglican church building, particularly in the Cardiff area. In 1920 the Anglican church in Wales was disestablished; since then the Church in Wales has been organised separately from the Church of England.

Baglan: St Catherine. 2 miles (3 km) north-west of Port Talbot.

This bold, red stone church, designed by John Prichard and consecrated in 1882, is one of the architect's best works. Cruciform in plan and Decorated Gothic in style, it has a tall pinnacled spire and a rich and elaborate interior. It is often referred to as the 'alabaster church' because of the extensive use inside of pink alabaster from Penarth. The arches have coloured voussoirs, the floors are mosaic and the reredos is of marble. The fine east window (Crucifixion) and the south transept window (St Cecilia) are by Burne-Jones. The ruins of the old church of St Baglan stand on the hill behind Baglan.

Bridgend: Old Meeting House (Elim Pentecostal Church), Park Street.

This is one of the earliest nonconformist chapels to survive in Glamorgan. It was built in 1795 to replace a Presbyterian chapel founded in 1672 by the Reverend Samuel Jones. In the course of the eighteenth century the congregation adopted Unitarian beliefs. It is typical of the earliest chapels in appearance and has two circular windows (now blocked) above the twin round-headed windows in the centre of the façade. It is now rented to the Pentecostal Church.

Cardiff: English Presbyterian Chapel, Windsor Place.

The ornate but graceful spire of this chapel provided one of the few vertical accents in the city centre before the coming of multi-storey office blocks. The chapel was built in 1866, to designs by Thomas Pilkington, for mainly Scottish Presbyterians. The curved bulges on either side of the building echo the original pseudo-circular shape of the interior before it was extended in 1893.

Cardiff: St German, Star Street, Roath.

St German's has the finest interior of any purely nineteenth-century church in Glamorgan. It was designed by G. F. Bodley and T. Garner and built between 1882 and 1884. The lofty interior, with its slender clusters of tall columns supporting a panelled wagon-vault roof, has a graceful simplicity and a soaring spaciousness that gives it a cathedral-like atmosphere. The tall nave windows are deeply set between internal buttresses. The chancel is large and has a flight of steps leading up to the high altar, behind which there is a splendid trio of tall lancet windows filled with stained glass designed by Bodley (1900). Wrought iron screens separate the chancel from two chapels, which are both roofed with graceful ribbed stone vaulting. Externally, apart from flying buttresses over the side chapels, the church is straightforward and unexceptional.

Cardiff: St John the Baptist.

St John's is Cardiff's only surviving city-centre medieval church. Its glory is the graceful three-stage Perpendicular-style tower topped by an exquisitely detailed openwork parapet and delicate lantern pinnacles. The church is entered through elegant ogee arches forming a porch at the base of the tower. The earliest record of the church is from the late twelfth century when it was a chapel of ease to St Mary's. The earliest parts now visible, however, are the early thirteenth-century arches on the south side of the chancel. In 1453 the church was almost completely rebuilt, possibly following damage in the Glyndwr rebellion. Twenty years later the superb tower was

added by John Hart to a commission by Anne, the wife of Richard III. In 1813 the church was restored and galleries were added, but these were removed in 1889-91 when the two outer aisles were added. Inside, the most interesting pre-Victorian part is the Herbert Chapel, separated from the chancel by a carved oak screen, with its seventeenth-century Jacobean monument to the Herbert brothers. The high-altar reredos is by Goscombe John and the south-aisle reredos and the east window are by Sir Ninian Comper.

Cardiff: St Mary, Bute Street, Butetown.

Since old St Mary's church had been washed away by the Taff in the seventeenth century there had been no church to serve the southern part of the town. With the rise of Cardiff as a port and a rapidly increasing population in the docks area, the need for a church soon became urgent. In order to raise money for a new church the poet William Wordsworth was induced to write a sonnet beseeching the builders to:
'Let the new Church be worthy of its aim
That in its beauty Cardiff may rejoice.'
John Foster, a Liverpool architect, responded with a vigorous and, for that time *avant-garde* design in quasi-Romanesque style. The new St Mary's was built with the aid of a parliamentary grant and opened in 1843. The exterior has an agreeably austere character with two square west towers topped by pyramidal roofs. Inside, the nave and two aisles are divided into five bays by massive round columns with Byzantine capitals supporting bold semicircular arched arcades, which in turn support a plain flat ceiling. At the west end a dark rib-vaulted apse was squeezed in between the two towers.

Cardiff: Tabernacle Baptist Chapel, The Hayes.

Tabernacle is one of Cardiff's three Welsh-language chapels. It was built in 1865, to designs by John Hartland, in an elegant Regency style. The main front, with its row of tall round-headed windows over an arcade of round-headed doorways, is recessed between two stair towers.

Cogan: St Peter. Off Sully Road, 1$^{1}/_{2}$ miles (2 km) south-west of Penarth.

This small church consists of a chancel, nave, south porch and bell turret. Much herringbone masonry can be seen on the north

Ewenny Priory, tomb slab of the founder.

and east sides, showing that this was one of the earliest Norman churches built in Glamorgan. The diminutive chancel arch is also Norman.

Coity: St Mary.

The large cruciform parish church is a fine early fourteenth-century building in Decorated Gothic style. There are no aisles and the interior is light and spacious. Under the low tower there is a groin-vaulted crossing. The stained glass of the east window, by the Morris firm, was installed in 1863. A very old carved oak chest in the chancel is thought to be a rare survival of a portable Easter sepulchre.

Cowbridge: The Holy Cross.

The parish church, near the centre of the town, is a large building in Early English and Perpendicular Gothic styles. The thirteenth-century central tower has a defensive look about it and is crowned by an eight-sided embattled parapet. Both the nave and the chancel have single aisles but the aisles are curiously arranged on opposite sides to each other, giving the interior an unbalanced appearance. Two of Glamorgan's best known historians, Rice Meyrick (died 1586) and Benjamin Malkin (1769-1842), are buried in the church. The church was restored in 1848.

Cowbridge: United Free Church (Ramoth Baptist Chapel).

This small but neat chapel is approached through an arched passageway from the busy High Street and stands at the end of a narrow, grave-lined lawn. It was built with tall windows and an almost pyramidal roof in 1828 to the designs of the chapel's own minister, the Reverend Thomas Morris. In its simplicity and lack of ostentation it represents a good example of early nonconformist architecture.

Ewenny: Priory Church of St Michael.

The Priory Church of St Michael stands at the end of a secluded rural lane and is one of the finest examples of early Norman church architecture in Wales; it is also an outstanding example of a fortified monastery. The church itself was founded about 1120 and later, in 1141, converted to a Benedictine priory by Maurice de Londres, lord of Ogmore. It comprises a long, early twelfth-century nave and a mid twelfth-century presbytery with a tower and transepts that were added a few decades later. The aisle and porch belong to the sixteenth century and the plain west wall was built in the nineteenth century when the nave was shortened. The roof over the nave (still in use as the parish church) is carried on great cylindrical piers, plain except for moulded bases and reeded capitals, and simple round arches. A thirteenth-century screen wall divides the parish church from the crossing, transepts and chancel, all now in the care of Cadw. The eastern section is the grandest and most dignified part of the building and includes the austere chancel with its simple barrel-vault ceiling subdivided by moulded ribs. A band of zigzag decoration marks the place where the walls were raised in height about 1200. The chancel is separated from the crossing by a fourteenth-century timber screen which may have originally been in the nave. The north transept has fallen in and is marked by low walls. The south transept has an interesting collection of monuments, including some early Christian headstones, and leads out through a Romanesque doorway into private gardens, where the monks' cloister was sited. Most of the monastic buildings have long since disappeared although fragments may have been incorporated within the mansion and its outbuildings alongside the church.

The priory is unusual in having a high perimeter wall defended with wall-walks, battlements, towers and gatehouses. The walls may have been erected for reasons of prestige rather than defence for they are strongest where they are most likely to impress but weakest where they would have been most vulnerable. Nevertheless, the north and south gates are solid enough and date back to the late twelfth century. The south-east tower was later converted to a dovecote.

Llancarfan: St Cadog. 5 miles (7 km) south-east of Cowbridge.

This large thirteenth-century church is set in an oval churchyard which may have been the site of the famous early Christian monastery founded by St Cadoc in the sixth century. The square piers which separate the nave and chancel from the south aisle and Raglan Chapel have sculptured capitals decorated with dog-tooth ornament. There is a large five-light sixteenth-century window in the chancel and a simple screen in the chapel which was probably the original rood-loft screen.

Llandaf Cathedral: St Peter and St Paul.

Although small when compared to the greater English cathedrals, Llandaf Cathedral is full of interest and what it lacks in size it more than makes up for in antiquity. The cathedral is hidden away from the village at the bottom of a hill and only its tall spire marks its position from a distance. Yet this is one of the oldest church sites in Britain, with a history going back to the early Christian saints of the sixth century. The earliest monastery, reputedly founded by St Teilo and probably built in timber, has disappeared without trace, as has the first small stone church, although a tenth-century cross in the south presbytery aisle is a reminder of this mysterious period. Since these rudimentary beginnings the cathedral has been rebuilt or restored five times. The first Norman cathedral was begun in 1120 by Bishop Urban and parts of his building can be seen in the arches in the presbytery and choir aisles. From about 1170 onward the church was largely rebuilt when the nave was extended westwards. North and south aisles were added during the thirteenth century, thus obscuring the original cruciform plan of the building. The exuberant Jasper Tower, with its elaborately decorated Perpendicular pinnacles, was added to the west end in the late fifteenth century. By the eighteenth century the cathe-

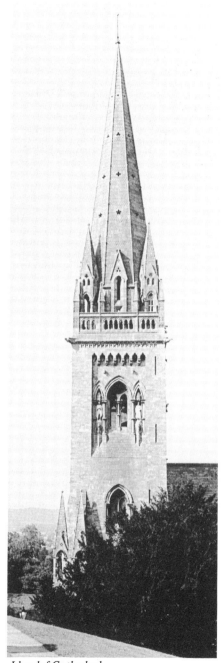

Llandaf Cathedral.

29

Llandaf Cathedral: the parabolic arch and organ case.

Llandough church and Irbic Cross.

dral had become derelict and one of the towers collapsed in 1723. Rather than rebuild the whole church, a classical-style temple, designed by John Wood the Elder of Bath, was erected within the ruins. During the next century the temple was demolished and the cathedral largely rebuilt by the local architect John Prichard. Prichard was responsible for sympathetically completing the west front and adding, in 1867, the splendid 195 foot (60 metre) high tower and spire at the south-west corner. During the Second World War the cathedral was bombed and once again lay in ruins; it was rebuilt and restored by George Pace between 1949 and 1960, during which time the David Chapel was also added.

In layout the cathedral is basically a simple rectangle of twelve bays with the Lady Chapel extending a further three bays at the east end. There are no transepts, but a small square chapter house (dating from 1240) with a pyramidal roof projects from the main building on the south side, while the David Chapel projects from the north side.

Inside, the most impressive part of the medieval building is the Romanesque chancel arch, which is richly decorated with bands of zigzag ornament and circlets enclosing flower emblems. The stained glass in the window above the arch is by John Piper. There are two fine Romanesque doorways in the south and north aisles. Beyond the chancel arch can be seen the delicate stone vaulting of the thirteenth-century Lady Chapel. Much of the dignified appearance of the interior is due to Prichard's careful restoration in the nineteenth century. Through the influence of Prichard's partner, John Seddon, many fine Pre-Raphaelite works of art were added. Notable amongst them is Rossetti's 'Seed of David' triptych in St Illtud's Chapel under the Jasper Tower. The deeply panelled flat timber ceiling is a modern alteration as also is the great parabolic concrete arch at the junction of the nave and choir. Surmounting the arch is a cylindrical organ case carrying an aluminium sculpture (by Sir Jacob Epstein) of Christ in Majesty. The Pre-Raphaelite gilded figures on the sides of the organ case originally stood in canopied niches above the choir stalls.

Llanddewi: St David. 14 miles (21 km) south-west of Swansea.

The church is sited on the brow of a hill amongst farm buildings. It has a low corbelled west tower with a transverse saddleback roof and is mostly of thirteenth-century date although there is a small Norman window on the north wall and it has a Norman tub font.

Llandough: St Dochdwy. On the B4267 road between Cardiff and Penarth.

The church, built in 1866 on the site of an earlier church and a Celtic monastery, has a tall saddleback tower and a polychromatic interior. The only reminder of the monastery is the very fine base of a pillar cross (late tenth or early eleventh century) standing in the churchyard. It is known as the Irbic Cross from an inscription, above a carving of a man on horseback, on the base of the pillar. The pillar is elaborately decorated with interlaced ropework patterns.

Llanmadoc: St Madog. 15 miles (24 km) west of Swansea.

This tiny thirteenth-century church has a curious, steeply pitched saddleback roof to the tower. It was heavily restored in 1861. A Romano-Celtic inscribed grave slab, dating from the fifth or sixth century, was discovered in the former rectory and subsequently reset in the sill of the east window. Two early Christian cross slabs (seventh to ninth century), which were found in the churchyard, have been reset in the nave.

Llantrisant: St Illtud, St Tyfodwg and St Gwynno.

The church is stoutly built and dominates the skyline of the hilltop when seen from a distance. The tower and western part were rebuilt in the early sixteenth century. In 1873 the church was restored and the nave arches 'gothicised'. At the same time the Crucifixion by Burne-Jones was incorporated in the east window. An early Christian grave slab in the south aisle dates from the seventh to ninth centuries and has three incised crosses. The octagonal font is Norman.

Llantwit Major: St Illtud.

The famous fifth-century Celtic monastery which once stood just north of the parish church has disappeared without trace. During the dark ages it became renowned as a centre of learning, attracting students from all over Wales and western England. The church is large and has an unusual straggling ground plan, reflecting its curious mixture of different periods. The western church was the original parish church, built on Norman, or perhaps

pre-Norman, foundations. It was largely rebuilt in the fifteenth century. In the thirteenth century a new (eastern, or collegiate) church with an aisled nave of four bays and a chancel was added to the east end of the western church and a tall slim tower inserted between the two buildings. A Lady Chapel, now in ruins, was added to the west end of the original building. Inside the eastern church there are traces of a number of medieval wall-paintings and, in the south aisle, a niche carved with a Jesse tree. The western church has a good timber roof and contains a remarkable collection of memorial stones and carved Celtic crosses, indicating, perhaps, the existence of a local school of sculptors. They include the elaborately decorated ninth-century Houelt wheel cross (probably a memorial to Hywel ap Rhys, king of Glywysing) and the tenth-century Samson stone commemorating another local king, shafts of two ninth-century pillar crosses and a tapering cylindrical pillar (tenth or eleventh century) decorated with plaitwork.

Margam: Abbey Church (dedication unknown).

Margam Abbey, founded by the Cistercians by 1147 on the site of a Celtic monastery, was

Church of St Illtud, Llantwit Major.

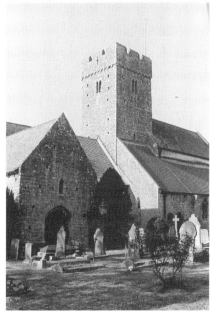

one of the largest and wealthiest monasteries in Wales. The eastern part is ruined but the nave is used as the parish church. The seven-bay nave with its massive piers was erected in the late twelfth century and has the austere lines usually associated with Cistercian architecture. The lower part of the Norman west front survives, including the Romanesque doorway and the three windows above, but the rest of the west front was rebuilt in Italianate style in 1805-10. Inside there are some good tombs of the Mansel family. The beautiful twelve-sided chapter house (which can be visited from Margam Park) was built in the thirteenth century; the central column supported elaborate vaulting branching out from the centre like a tree, and even in partial ruin it remains an elegant structure.

The **Margam Stones Museum** (telephone: 0222 465511), in the old village school just to the north of the church, houses a large collection of early Christian inscribed stones and Celtic crosses. Five of the crosses, including the great ninth- or tenth-century cross of Conbelin, come from Margam itself and are evidence of a pre-Norman religious foundation on the site. Possibly there was also a school of sculptors at Margam. One of the larger stones was rediscovered in 1698 in use as a footbridge! Another stone had originally been in use as a Roman milestone but was recut in the sixth century.

Merthyr Mawr: St Teilo. 2 miles (3 km) south-west of Bridgend.

This delightful little church, rebuilt in 1849-51, is pleasantly sited in a picturesque estate village. Early English in style and well detailed, it has an unusual lantern turret at the west end. Both Benjamin Ferrey and John Prichard appear to have participated in the design of the church. A number of inscribed stones and early Christian cross slabs have been collected together on the north side of the churchyard.

Merthyr Tydfil: St Tydful.

In 1809 the Bishop of Llandaf wrote: 'I went over the mountains to a place where no bishop had ever held a confirmation before, Merthyr Tydfil.' Twenty years later the fourteenth-century parish church was taken down and a new Romanesque-style church erected in its place. The new church was much larger and had galleries to cater for the fast-growing population of the town. In 1895 the church was radically altered by J. L. Pearson. The

well proportioned and spacious interior has a flat ceiling over the nave but vaulting over the aisles and is apse-ended.

Morriston: Tabernacle Chapel.

Referred to sometimes as 'the great cathedral of Welsh nonconformity', Tabernacle is, with its soaring spire and boldly arcaded classical front, the most striking of all Welsh chapels in appearance. The interior has an impressive gallery which curves down towards the pulpit, stained glass windows and a panelled ceiling. It is also the largest chapel in Wales, with seating for 1800, and cost £18,000 to build in 1873. The architect was John Humphreys, who, together with the minister and builder, visited many chapels in England to study their construction and cull ideas for attractive features to use on Tabernacle.

Neath: Abbey Church of the Holy Trinity. See chapter 4.

Neath: St David.

Another bold Victorian church, St David's was built in 1864-6 to designs by John Norton. It has a lofty tower, 152 feet (46 metres) high, topped by a pinnacled spire, transepts, an aisled nave and an apsidal chancel. The exterior is in local blue sandstone with bands of red sandstone, but the interior is of red and black brickwork.

Oxwich: St Illtud. 11 miles (18 km) south-west of Swansea.

The church, beautifully sited in an unspoilt setting close to the sea, is mainly of twelfth-century date. The tiny cell-like chancel may, however, be pre-Norman. The large embattled tower was added in the fourteenth century. Oil lamps and a simple interior help to give the church its atmosphere of antiquity. There is a fine ogee-arched recess in the north wall of the chancel containing recumbent effigies of a knight and his lady. The ceiling in the chancel was decorated in 1931 by Leslie Young, scenic artist of Sadlers Wells Theatre.

Penarth: St Augustine.

Penarth's architectural glory is St Augustine's church, which stands on the hill above the town and overlooks the sea. It replaced a medieval church and was built in 1866 to designs by William Butterfield, a celebrated church architect in his day. Butterfield designed his churches in functional Gothic rather

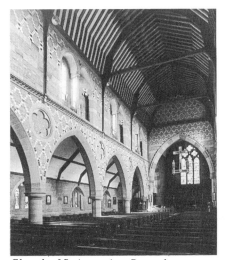

Church of St Augustine, Penarth.

than in a revived medieval Gothic style. He was the originator of 'polychromatic architecture' and by his imaginative use of multicoloured brickwork laid to geometrical patterns he produced some outstanding interiors. St Augustine's is no exception. The exterior of the church is built in grey-white limestone and its tall eye-catching tower, 90 feet (27 metres) high, has a saddleback roof in keeping with the original medieval church, in order, so it is said, to conform to Admiralty charts. For the lofty interior Butterfield used yellow Bath stone and pink sandstone for the nave columns and arch surrounds, but raw red brickwork filled with black and white diaperwork for the walls above, to produce an unusual but dramatic space, full of warmth and light, in marked contrast to the bleak but imposing exterior.

Pontardawe: Gellionen Unitarian Chapel. 1½ miles (2 km) west of Pontardawe at OS 170: SN 701042.

A chapel for the Society of Protestant Dissenters was first erected on this isolated and windswept moorland site in 1692. The present building was built in 1801 in typical early nonconformist style, with two tall round-headed windows in the centre of the main façade and doors at either end, one for men and one for women and children. There is a large graveyard attached and, nearby, ruins of the stable for the minister's horse.

Pontypridd: Pontypridd Historical and Cultural Centre (Capel Tabernacl). Telephone: 0443 402077.

This Baptist chapel, situated next to the famous old bridge, was built in 1861 to the designs of the chapel's own minister, Dr E. Roberts. It has a strongly detailed pediment and is a good example of classically influenced chapel architecture at its best. The chapel has now been imaginatively converted to a heritage centre.

Port Talbot: Beulah Chapel. Just off A4211 near Margam Groes.

This delightful octagonal chapel, the only one in Wales, was built in 1838 on land at Margam Groes given by C. R. M. Talbot of Margam Abbey, on condition that it was built to his own design. The inspiration for the plan was possibly that of the chapter house at Margam Abbey, but the elevational design is more Italianate than Gothic. The chapel was taken down and rebuilt on its present site to make way for the nearby motorway.

Rhosili: St Mary. 18 miles (29 km) west of Swansea.

The original twelfth-century church dedicated to St Fili was sited at the Warren near the beach but was abandoned when it became engulfed by sand. The present church, standing above the clifftop, was probably built in the thirteenth century. It consists of chancel, nave, south porch and a plain saddleback west tower. The ornate Romanesque south doorway is thought to have come from the original church. On the south side of the chancel there is a 'leper' window. The memorial tablet on the north wall of the nave is to Petty Officer Edgar Evans RN, who died on the tragic journey back from the South Pole with Captain Scott in 1912.

Rhymney: St David.

St David's was probably the last neo-classical church to be built in Wales and has a closer affinity with the nonconformist chapels of the valleys than with the Anglican churches. It is well proportioned and has a square east tower and round-headed windows. It was designed by Philip Hardwick in 1839, erected at the expense of the Rhymney Iron Company, and consecrated in 1843.

St Donat's: St Donat. 2¹/₄ miles (3.5 km) west of Llantwit Major.

The little parish church is hidden away in a wooded dingle below the castle walls. Although built by the Normans, possibly on the site of a Celtic church, the building has a fifteenth-century appearance, largely due to the Perpendicular windows inserted in that period and the corbelled parapets to the nave and the west tower. Inside, the Norman origins of the present church can be seen in the low round-headed chancel arch and the heavily moulded font. The chancel was probably added in the fourteenth century but was drastically restored during the nineteenth century. The Lady Chapel, standing on the north side of the chancel, was rebuilt by Sir Thomas Stradling in the sixteenth century; it contains some good monuments to the Stradling family, including three unusual paintings on wood. In the churchyard there is a fine late fifteenth-century Calvary cross decorated with carvings of the Crucifixion and the Virgin Mary.

Swansea: Mount Pleasant Chapel, St Helen's Road.

This fine classical-style Baptist chapel was built in 1875 to the designs of George Morgan to replace an earlier building (now the Sunday school), which still stands alongside. It is fronted by a majestic Corinthian portico added in 1885.

Swansea: St Paul, Sketty.

This is the best of Swansea's many Anglican churches. It was built in 1849-52 to designs by Henry Woodyer which convincingly attempt to recreate the atmosphere of an old parish church. The 100 foot (30 metre) high broach spire is clad in oak shingles and there is a good timber porch. The church was enlarged in 1908.

Mount Pleasant Chapel, Swansea.

Beaupre Castle, St Hilary.

6
Historic houses and gardens

Compared with other parts of Wales, the fertile lowlands of Glamorgan have given rise to a rich heritage of gentry houses. With the coming of more peaceful conditions after the middle ages strong fortified houses became unnecessary. The development of new types of house to take their place was, however, slow and much of the character of the greater postmedieval houses in Glamorgan was derived from castle architecture. The main building period seems to have been the sixteenth and seventeenth centuries. After that the pace of building slackened, probably because there were by then sufficient large houses to meet the needs of the gentry. The next great building period coincided with the industrial revolution when many of the *nouveaux riches* decided to erect houses in keeping with their new status. Often they turned back to the middle ages for their architectural inspiration, sometimes with dramatic results. Even more dramatic were the idiosyncratic restorations

carried out for Lord Bute at Cardiff Castle (see chapter 4) and Castell Coch during the latter part of the nineteenth century; they have little to equal them anywhere else in Britain.

Beaupre Castle, St Hilary. Telephone: 04463 3034. Cadw.

Beaupre Castle is hidden away on the edge of a secluded valley in the heart of the Vale of Glamorgan. The original house belonged to the Bassets and was built around a south-facing courtyard (now gone) in the early fourteenth century. In the sixteenth century Beaupre passed to Sir Rice Mansel of Oxwich and he transformed the house by extending it northwards and adding a courtyard on this side. The later courtyard is entered through a grand gatehouse built in 1586 with a mixture of late Gothic windows and early Renaissance surrounds. Above the Tudor doorway is the coat of arms of the Bassets. On the opposite side of the courtyard there is a magnificent three-

Castell Coch, Tongwynlais: banqueting hall (left) and drawing room (right).

storey porch which was added to the earlier building in 1600. The ornate porch was designed in a flamboyant 'Italian' manner with three superimposed pairs of classical columns; above the Tudor doorway there is another elaborate coat of arms.

Castell Coch, Tongwynlais, Cardiff. Telephone: 0222 810101. Cadw.

Although Castell Coch was exotically restored and revamped in the nineteenth century it is still basically the fortress built by Gilbert de Clare in the thirteenth century to guard the entrance to the Taff Gorge. Perched high up on the side of a steep hill, the castle occupies the site of an earlier Welsh stronghold built in the mid twelfth century by Ifor ap Meurig, lord of Senghenydd. Its unusual triangular layout, with three circular towers capped by conical roofs, gives it the romantic appearance of a Rhineland castle. Between 1875 and the 1890s the castle was restored and the upper parts were completely rebuilt by William Burges for Lord Bute. As far as possible Burges rebuilt the outer parts in what he considered to

be an appropriately thirteenth-century style. The exterior is therefore, apart from the questionable, but delightful, conical roofs, a fairly sober reconstruction of a medieval castle. Burges even included a working drawbridge complete with portcullis at the entrance. This leads into a small, but convincingly atmospheric, courtyard encircled by towers, galleries and apartments.

Inside the apartment wing and keep tower all is different. Here Burges indulged in a sumptuous extravaganza of Victorian decoration and invention which were equalled only by the same architect's interiors at Cardiff Castle (see chapter 4). Steps lead up to the first-floor banqueting hall, which is decorated with scenes of saints and martyrs and has a heavily sculpted fireplace. Next comes the octagonal drawing room, a wonderful two-storey space with an encircling balcony and a colourful rib-vaulted ceiling; the walls are exuberantly decorated with scenes from Aesop's *Fables*. A spiral staircase leads up to the rather more restrained bedroom of Lord Bute and on again to Lady Bute's bedroom, another splendid room with a domed ceiling and profusely decorated. In complete contrast are the functional portcullis room above the entrance gate and the bare-walled cellar, lit only by rays of light from two tiny holes, at the bottom of the tower. Outside the castle long walks are possible in the surrounding forest.

Clyne Gardens and Clyne Country Park, Mumbles Road, Blackpill, Swansea. Telephone enquiries: Swansea City Council, 0792 302420.

The gardens were originally laid out as an estate park for Clyne Castle (now a hostel belonging to the University College of Swansea). The gardens fill a small winding valley which slopes steeply down towards the sea and offers superb views overlooking Swansea Bay. There are splendid collections of azaleas, magnolias and camellias, best seen in late spring and early summer. Clyne Castle can be seen on the northern side of the gardens. It was built as a modest country house, known as Woodlands, in 1791, extended in 1800 and then remodelled in Gothic style in 1819-20. The adjacent country park extends over 650 acres (260 ha) of woodland and has walks, cycleways, picnic sites and an adventure play area. The picturesque 'Ivy Tower' was part of

the main chimney-stack of the short-lived Clyne Wood Copper Works built in the valley between 1825 and 1840. The Clyne Valley Canal of 1799-1803 skirts the lower part of the country park.

Cyfarthfa Castle, Brecon Road, Merthyr Tydfil CF47 8RE. Telephone: 0685 723112.

Grandly conceived in castellated medieval style with battlemented towers, the 'castle' was the stronghold of an industrial ironmaster rather than a feudal chieftain and represented a romantic escape back to another age. At a distance the ruggedness of the building looks convincing but from close to the over-large windows reveal its falseness. It was built in 1825 to designs by Richard Lugar for the ironmaster William Crawshay II on a hilly site overlooking the famous Cyfarthfa Ironworks, then the largest in Britain. It is surrounded by a 160 acre (66 ha) park and looks on to a small lake. Much has changed since the days of the great ironmasters and the mansion is now partly a museum (see chapter 7) and partly a school.

Dyffryn Gardens, St Nicholas, near Cardiff CF5 6SU. Telephone: 0222 593328.

The gardens were laid out for John Cory by

Cyfarthfa Castle, Merthyr Tydfil.

the landscape gardener Thomas Mawson at the beginning of the twentieth century around Dyffryn House, a late nineteenth-century mansion built in the style of a French *château* and now used as a conference centre. The gardens were further developed by Reginald Cory and have become one of the finest botanic centres in Wales. In front of the mansion there are handsome lawns bisected by a lily canal with fountains at one end. Around these lawns are woods and rock and heather gardens on the east side and a variety of smaller, individually designed gardens in different styles, including a Roman garden, a rose garden, sunken gardens and a fountain court, on the west side. On the other side of Dyffryn House there are greenhouses with collections of cacti, ferns and orchids and a large temperate and palm house.

Llancaiach-fawr, Nelson, near Ystrad Mynach. Telephone: 0443 815588.

Llancaiach-fawr is an excellent example of a stoutly built mansion erected in the upland area during unsettled times, when a gentry house needed to be a stronghold as well as a home. It was built in the early sixteenth century for the Prichard family and, apart from a few modifications in the seventeenth century,

has survived little altered. It is a tall dour-looking three-storey L-shaped house with a two-storey entrance porch. The absence of large windows at ground-floor level and the massive battered walls help to give the house its defensive character. The main staircase, added in the seventeenth century, just inside the porch, leads to the three principal rooms on the first floor. Inside, the heavily built door-ways between rooms and the large number of staircases constructed within the thickness of the walls, some possibly intended as escape routes, reflect how security-conscious the builders of the house were. The sixteenth-century bard Dafydd Benwyn wrote a poem praising the splendour of Llancaiach.

Margam Park, Margam, Port Talbot SA13 2TJ. Telephone: 0639 881635.

This vast 800 acre (320 ha) estate park has something to attract almost everyone. Orig-inally part of the monastic estate of Margam Abbey and then, after the dissolution of the monastery, the park of Margam House, seat of the Mansels, and of Margam Castle, the seat of the Talbots, it was eventually acquired by the county council and transformed into a country park. The park retains a herd of fallow deer, as well as a few red deer, and there are a

Dyffryn Gardens, St Nicholas.

The orangery, Margam Park.

farm trail and a number of waymarked hill trails of varying length starting from the visitor centre near the ruins of Margam Castle. A fine outdoor collection of contemporary sculpture is dotted around the park and there are also picnic sites, an adventure playground, a maze and a children's village (for those under eight). Margam Castle, designed by Thomas Hopper to give the impression of the accumulated construction of centuries but in reality built in five years between 1830 and 1835, was ruined in a great fire but still impresses by its sheer size. Dominated by a great octagonal tower in the centre, the Tudor-style mansion is a vigorous mixture of pinnacles, chimneys, gables, crenellated parapets and buttresses.

The famous **Orangery**, the longest in Britain at 327 feet (100 metres), is lower down the hill near Margam Abbey. It is an elegant building, designed in classical style by Anthony Keck, with rows of tall round-headed windows. It was built in 1787 to protect the orange and lemon trees which, according to tradition, were part of a shipwrecked present sent to King George III from Portugal. Close by is the chapter house belonging to the abbey (see chapter 5). The foundations of the original village of Margam have been excavated in the area west of the Orangery. Also in this area is a gardeners' museum and the seventeenth-century classical-style façade of the Summer Banqueting House.

Oxwich Castle, Oxwich. Cadw.

The conservation of Oxwich castle is nearing completion but meanwhile it can be seen from the surrounding area. It is not really a castle, although possibly built on the site of one, but rather a large and imposing Tudor mansion arranged around two sides of a courtyard. The west wall of the courtyard has been partly destroyed but the mock-military gateway which led into the enclosure still survives; above the gate is the coat of arms of Sir Rice Mansel sculpted in stone. The two-storey south block was probably built by Sir Rice about 1520-38, but the splendid and larger east block was the work of his son, Sir Edward Mansel, between 1559 and 1580. The east block is a remarkable building, four storeys high on the main front but with six-storey projecting wings at the rear. Although much ruined, the large first-floor hall and the elegant long gallery at third-floor level can easily be made out. The large circular dovecote at the north end of the east block dates from an earlier period.

St Donat's Castle, St Donat's, near Llantwit Major CF6 9WF. Telephone: 0446 792271.

The castle has been in continuous occupation since the late thirteenth century when Peter de Stradling, a Swiss knight, married Joan de Hawey, a Norman heiress. It remained in the hands of the Stradlings and their heirs for more than four centuries until 1738, when Sir Thomas Stradling was killed in a duel. The castle passed to the Tyrwhits and was later sold, in 1901, to Morgan Williams of Aberpergwm, who carried out considerable alterations. It was sold again in 1925 to Randolph Hearst, the American newspaper magnate, who incorporated various medieval structures and details into the fabric of the building. In 1969 St Donat's Castle became the home of Atlantic College, the first international sixth-form college in the world. Although the castle has undergone many changes, alterations and additions to meet the needs of its various owners, it still retains the form of a concentrically planned fortress with its inner bailey protected by strong curtain walls and a rock-cut ditch. The outer gatehouse is defended by a drawbridge and portcullis, but the inner gate is simply an opening in the curtain wall. The inner courtyard of the castle has the character of a Tudor mansion as a result of reconstruction and additions carried out during the Elizabethan or early Jacobean period. The great hall dates from the fifteenth century and still retains its original chimneypiece and ceiling. The fourteenth-century roof and windows of the Bradenstoke Hall, behind the great hall, were brought from Bradenstoke Priory in Wiltshire in 1937 and re-erected here. The impressive timber ceiling in the dining hall was brought to St Donat's from a Lincolnshire church. Below the castle there are terraced gardens reaching down to the coast.

St Fagans Castle, St Fagans, Cardiff CF5 6XB. Telephone: 0222 569441.

Whitewashed St Fagans Castle is a typical Elizabethan mansion, with its symmetrical E-plan main front and its many high gables. It was built by Dr John Gibbon about 1580 within the curtain walls of an abandoned thirteenth-century castle. It is now the centre-piece of the Welsh Folk Museum (see chapter 7). All the rooms on the two lower floors, and including the long gallery, have been richly furnished with seventeenth-century furniture collected from different parts of Wales. There are extensive formal gardens on both sides of the house. Those on the main front include a mulberry grove, a rose garden, a herb garden and a knot garden. The gardens on the west side are beautifully laid out in a series of terraces stepping down to a delightful little valley filled with a chain of eighteenth-century fishponds.

St Fagans Castle.

National Museum of Wales, Cardiff.

Museums

CARDIFF

Museum of 1st The Queen's Dragoon Guards, The Castle, Cardiff CF1 2RB. Telephone: 0222 222253.

This museum occupies the upper floor of the curtain wall east of the main entrance to the castle. Three galleries have excellent displays of arms, medals and uniforms as well as tableaux relating to the fortunes of the Dragoon Guards from 1685 until the present day. The Dragoon Guards, unofficially known as the Cavalry Regiment of Wales, is now an armoured reconnaissance regiment.

National Museum of Wales, Cathays Park, Cardiff CF1 3NP. Telephone: 0222 397951.

The National Museum was opened in 1927 and has since expanded to include specialist museums all over Wales. The main building is an architectural masterpiece in its own right,

the marble columns and floors of its monumental entrance hall glowing with a suffused pink light from the dome high above. On either side of the entrance hall are various exhibition galleries. Those on the lower floors are devoted to natural history and have imaginative displays dealing with animal, bird and plant life as well as large collections of rocks, minerals and fossils. The upper-floor galleries are devoted to art and archaeology. The refurbished east wing houses the Welsh national art collection. Welsh artists, including Richard Wilson and Augustus and Gwen John, feature prominently but there is also an exceptionally fine collection of French Impressionist and Post-Impressionist works and a gallery devoted to tapestry cartoons by Rubens. There is also a large collection of ceramics. The archaeology section includes finds from prehistoric, Roman, Celtic and medieval Wales and has an impressive display of early Christian crosses and a fine collection of coins and medals. Temporary exhibitions are held regularly in the entrance hall. There is a restaurant and bookshop.

The Welch Regiment Museum of the Royal Regiment of Wales (41st/69th Foot), The Castle, Cardiff CF1 2RB. Telephone: 0222 229367.

The museum, housed in three floors of the Black and Barbican Towers of Cardiff Castle, depicts the turbulent history of the regiment in the period 1719-1969 and its strong military and social links with South Wales through the associated Corps of Militia and Volunteers. The first twenty years of service of the Royal Regiment of Wales are also depicted by a fine collection of military colours, insignia, uniforms and militaria. In the Waterloo Room (the windlass room of the castle) there are six stained glass windows from the Wavell Memorial Chapel, Aldershot.

Welsh Industrial and Maritime Museum, Bute Street, Cardiff CF1 6AN. Telephone: 0222 481919.

The museum aims to tell the story of how industry, road, rail and sea transport evolved in Wales. It is housed in five separate buildings near the former pierhead. The main building is a modern, industrial-looking structure standing on the site of the old Merchants' Exchange, one of Cardiff's two exchanges dating from the city's heyday as the world's busiest coal port. The Hall of Power contains displays of different types of engines (many of which are operational) used in industry. Outside exhibits include a working replica of Trevithick's steam locomotive used at Penydarren in 1804 (see chapter 8). A nearby **Transport Gallery** has a collection of trams, buses, bicycles and cars from the earliest days. Other parts of the museum are housed in original dockland buildings. The **Shipping Gallery** in Stuart Street is in the old P. and A. Campbell's steamer booking office and has models, artefacts and a video show to illustrate the history of sea-borne passenger travel. The **Railway Gallery** is in the former terminus and head office of the Taff Vale Railway at the old Bute Road Station (see chapter 8). Inside there is a collection of models while outside old steam locomotives are being restored. **126 Bute Street** was formerly a ship chandlery; it has displays telling the story of Cardiff Docks and a recreation of a dockland street.

CRYNANT
Cefn Coed Colliery Museum, Blaenant Colliery, Crynant, Neath SA10 8SN. Telephone: 0639 750556. 5 miles (8 km) north of Neath on A4109.

The museum is housed in former buildings of the Cefn Coed Colliery. When the mine was sunk in 1926 it was considered to be the deepest anthracite coal mine in Britain with shafts 2300 feet (690 metres) deep. The colliery closed in 1968 and the surface workings were incorporated with the adjoining Blaenant Mine, which closed in 1990. The exhibits include a massive steam winding engine, a colliery locomotive and a recreated mining gallery.

CYNONVILLE
Welsh Miners Museum, Afan Argoed Country Park, Cynonville, Port Talbot SA13 3HL. Telephone: 0639 850564. On A4107 between Port Talbot and Cymmer.

Mining as seen through the eyes of miners is the theme of the displays, which include a traditional miner's cottage scene, simulated underground mining and early mining equipment. The hardships and struggles of this dangerous and dirty job and the story of children working underground are well brought out.

Welsh Industrial and Maritime Museum, Cardiff: Trevithick's engine.

KNELSTON
Gower Farm Trail and Farm Museum. See chapter 2.

MARGAM
Margam Stones Museum. See chapter 5, under Margam: Abbey Church.

MERTHYR TYDFIL
Cyfarthfa Castle Museum and Art Gallery, Brecon Road, Merthyr Tydfil CF47 8RE. Telephone: 0685 723112.

The museum is housed in a wing of the 'castle' (see chapter 6) and includes displays of social history, natural history, geology, industrial history and some unexpected relics from ancient Egypt. The extensive fine art collections range from nineteenth-century industrial scenes to works by modern artists. Of particular interest is the fine collection of watercolours by Penry Williams, a native of Merthyr Tydfil, who was patronised by the Crawshay family. In the basement there is a major gallery on Merthyr Tydfil.

Ynysfach Engine House. See chapter 8.

NEATH
Neath Borough Museum, Church Place, Neath. Telephone: 0639 645741.

This small but very pleasant museum is housed in the former Mechanics' Institute. A plaque records that it was built in 1847 to the designs of Alfred Russell Wallace, a local surveyor and naturalist who is best known for his studies concerning the theory of evolution and the law of natural selection. The ground floor is devoted to temporary exhibitions while the first-floor gallery is mainly concerned with the Roman period and local natural history.

PENARTH
Turner House Art Gallery, Plymouth Road, Penarth. Telephone: 0222 708870.

The building was erected in 1888 by James Pyke Thompson as a private art gallery and was named in memory of the painter J. M. W. Turner. It is now a branch of the National Museum of Wales and displays paintings, period furniture and *objets d'art*, as well as temporary exhibitions, all in an atmosphere of elegant informality.

PONTYPRIDD
Pontypridd Historical and Cultural Centre. See chapter 5.

PORTHCAWL
Porthcawl Museum, Old Police Station, John Street, Porthcawl. Telephone: 065671 6639.

This is a local history museum run on a voluntary basis and open in the afternoons. It is housed in the cells and offices of the old police station, which was converted into a museum and information centre in 1977.

RHOOSE
Wales Aircraft Museum, Cardiff-Wales Airport, Rhoose, near Barry CF6 9EU. Telephone: 0446 710135.

The open-air museum is situated on the approach road to the airport. Nearly thirty aircraft and helicopters, including an Avro Vulcan bomber, and other aviation relics are on display. Refreshments are served in an old Vickers Viscount airliner. The airport itself was originally built as a wartime training airfield in 1942. It was opened for civil flying in 1952.

ST FAGANS
Welsh Folk Museum, St Fagans, Cardiff CF5 6XB. Telephone: 0222 569441. 4 miles (6 km) west of Cardiff.

Anyone interested in the social history or traditional life and culture of Wales should visit this 100 acre (40 ha) museum, which was established in the grounds of St Fagans Castle (see chapter 6) in 1946 through the benevolence of Lord Plymouth. It is in two parts. The first part is a modern museum building constructed around an open courtyard. Agricultural vehicles are exhibited in an open colonnaded area near the entrance. From the spacious entrance hall the visitor can walk through various galleries and see items ranging from love spoons to ploughs. There are displays relating to domestic life, costume, agriculture, medicine, education and religion. There are also a bookshop and a restaurant in the building.

The second part of the museum is a folk park where the physical background to Welsh life has been painstakingly recreated. Here there are carefully rebuilt industrial and agricultural cottages and farms from all parts of Wales, a woollen factory, a tannery and a smithy from Powys, a cockpit from Clwyd, a pottery and a shop from Glamorgan, a gorse mill from Gwynedd, and a corn mill, bakehouse, tollgate house, school and eighteenth-century chapel from Dyfed. The woollen mill, corn mill and smithy are all working buildings where craftsmen still carry on their traditional work; other craftsmen display their skills in different parts of the museum.

SEVEN SISTERS

Seven Sisters Museum and Sawmills, 7 Dulais Road, Seven Sisters, Neath SA10 9EL. Telephone: 0639 700288. 11 miles (16 km) north of Neath on A4109.

A modern sawmill at work and old tools and machines illustrate the changes in woodworking methods. A large collection of mining lamps depicts their evolution from the eighteenth century to the present. Also in the grounds is 'Gunsmoke', a children's cowboy town and adventure playground.

SWANSEA

Glynn Vivian Art Gallery, Alexandra Road, Swansea SA1 5DZ. Telephone: 0792 655006 or 651738.

The Glynn Vivian Art Gallery was opened in 1911 with money donated by Richard Glynn Vivian. Originally it was used to house Vivian's personal collection of art and crafts of varying quality. Since then the miscellany has been added to considerably and the gallery now contains fine collections of paintings, including works by Swansea-born Ceri Richards, and of British and continental china and glass. The most prized possessions are perhaps the exquisite examples of Swansea pottery and porcelain which were made during a brief period early in the nineteenth century. There is a sculpture court and there is also a programme of exhibitions and events throughout the year.

Swansea Maritime and Industrial Museum, Maritime Quarter, Swansea SA1 1SN. Telephone: 0792 650351 or 470371.

The museum is housed in an old Coast Lines warehouse (built about 1900) in an exciting location alongside the old South Dock, where a number of historic vessels are moored. The museum is intended to illustrate the development of industry in Swansea from its agricultural beginnings to the present day. Inside the vast building there is, on the ground floor, a good transport collection including horse-drawn vehicles, cars, lorries and motorcycles. Upstairs there is a large collection of ship models. The major exhibit upstairs, however, is the Abbey Woollen Mill, which was brought from Neath and rehoused in the museum. The mill is still in production and traditional Welsh

Welsh Folk Museum, St Fagans: pottery and tannery.

Swansea Museum.

blankets and shawls are on sale. A tramshed houses a restored Swansea tram and relics of the old Mumbles Railway, including the cab of the last tram to operate on the line.

Swansea Museum, Victoria Road, Swansea SA1 1SN. Telephone: 0792 653763.

This is the oldest museum in Wales, having been founded in 1835 by the Royal Institution of South Wales. The present building was opened in 1841. Behind its imposing Ionic portico, the museum maintains its traditional layout and atmosphere. There are collections of local archaeology, Egyptology, Swansea and Nantgarw china and natural history (including reputedly the last golden eagle from the Brecon Beacons); also a reconstructed Welsh kitchen and an exhibition devoted to the industry of the Lower Swansea Valley. There is a good display of eighteenth- and nineteenth-century local topographical drawings and watercolours, and a large collection of photographs from the 1840s.

Robertstown Tramroad Bridge, Aberdare.

8
Industrial history

Glamorgan is rich in the remains of industrial history despite numerous reclamation projects that have taken place in the county. The industries associated with the county's past are chiefly metallurgy and mining and it was these heavy industries which led to the enormous growth in population between the late seventeenth century and the early twentieth century. Allied to these industries was the extraordinary network of canals, roads and railways which linked them to the chain of old and new ports on the southern coast; from these ports the metals and coal were exported all over the world.

The chief centres of the metallurgical smelting industries were Neath and Swansea and at one time 90 per cent of Britain's copper was smelted in West Glamorgan. An excellent handbook to the *Industrial Archaeology of the Swansea Region*, in which nearly two hundred sites are listed, has been published by the Royal Commission on Ancient and Historic Monuments in Wales. Although a number of towns had their own ironworks, the iron industry was dominated by Merthyr Tydfil, which had vast undertakings employing many thousands of workers and was, for a time, the world's iron 'capital'. The Merthyr Tydfil Heritage Trust has done much to reawaken interest in the town's industrial history and has produced a number of publications dealing

with it (obtainable at Ynysfach Engine House). Coal mining, which for a century and a half dominated the life of the valleys, is now in decline and few of the collieries are still worked. The coal-mining sites are still very much in evidence, however, and a number of walks in the coalfield are arranged by the Welsh Miners Museum, Cynonville (see chapter 7).

Many of the county's more interesting industrial sites have been abandoned for years and have not been maintained; great care should be taken by visitors to these. The following sites are a few of the best and most easily accessible of the many industrial sites in Glamorgan.

Aberdare: Cwm Dare Industrial Trail, Gadlys (OS 170: SN 999027).

This 2 mile (3 km) long trail starts at the site of the old Gadlys Colliery (sunk 1844) and then follows the line of the Dare Valley Railway (built 1866) through the Dare Valley Country Park to the existing buildings of the Bwllfa Dare Colliery. The Dare Valley Railway was crossed by a magnificent viaduct, the last of Brunel's timber viaducts to survive, which carried a branch of the Vale of Neath Railway. The viaduct was demolished in 1947 and only the masonry supporting piers still stand. The Bwllfa Dare Colliery was reconstructed in

1948-53 to connect with and form an entrance to Maerdy Colliery in the Rhondda Fach valley.

Aberdare: Robertstown Tramroad Bridge, Trecynon (OS 170: SN 997037).

This elegant cast iron bridge was erected across the Afon Cynon in 1811 to carry the tramroad linking the local ironworks with the Glamorganshire Canal. It is supported on four slim trussed arches and still retains the metal decking specially ribbed to prevent horses slipping.

Aberdulais Falls, Aberdulais, Neath SA10 8EU (OS 170: SS 772995). Telephone: 0639 636674. National Trust.

Although this was probably the site of the sixteenth-century copper works and was subsequently used as a corn mill and for ironworking, the visible remains are of the tinplate works founded in 1830. The upper part of the tinplate works was situated near the waterfall, which also provided the power, and lasted until about 1890; elevated walkways provide visitors with views of the remains, which include foundations of furnaces, a weir, header tank, wheel pit and a 60 foot (18 metre) high stack. The lower works were further south, on the left bank of the river, and continued to produce tinplate until 1939. A visitor centre (in the old stables) houses displays relating to the history of the site as well as reproductions of paintings of the waterfall by nineteenth-century artists.

Cardiff: Bute Road Railway Station, Bute Street (OS 170: ST 191748). Telephone: 0222 481919.

The three-storey building with hipped roof and tall chimneys was formerly the headquarters of the Taff Vale Railway Company and terminus of their line from Merthyr Tydfil. It was built about 1842 and is thus one of the earliest purpose-built railway buildings still standing. The ground floor now houses the Railway Gallery of the Welsh Industrial and Maritime Museum (see chapter 7). The building is also the headquarters of the Butetown Historic Railway Society, which is creating a Wales Railway centre alongside, where locomotives and other rolling stock are being restored.

Cardiff: Old Pumping Station, Penarth Road (OS 171: ST 160752).

The yellow and red brick basilica-like pumping station was built in 1901 to deal with sewage on the west side of Cardiff and was powered by an early form of incinerator plant burning domestic rubbish. It was closed in 1975 and has since been converted to a 'Victorian' street with antique shops and craft workshops.

Flat Holm Lighthouse and fortifications (OS 171: ST 222647). Flat Holm is accessible by boat (three or four sailings a week in summer) from Barry. Telephone: Flat Holm Project, 0446 747661.

Flat Holm's 165 foot (50 metre) high lighthouse, lying at the southern end of the island, was one of the last in Britain to be privately owned, but it was taken over by Trinity House in 1823. The island lies in the midst of busy shipping lanes but the lighthouse was not built until 1737. In 1820 the coal-fired brazier which originally provided the light was replaced by an oil-burning lamp. In 1969 the light was converted to electricity.

Between 1865 and 1869 Flat Holm was fortified with gun batteries at each corner of the island as part of Lord Palmerston's defence system for the Bristol Channel. Each of the four batteries consisted of one, two or three circular gun-pits housing 7 inch (175 mm) cannon. The cannon were mounted on Moncrieff carriages, which were designed to disappear out of sight below the rim of the gun-pit each time the gun was fired. The gun-pits, handsomely built in ashlared limestone, remain and some of the cannon are lying around, but the carriages have all gone. Like other fortresses on the English south coast, the guns were never used and the fortresses became known as 'Palmerston's Follies'.

During the Second World War the island was refortified. Two new batteries, each comprising concrete gun shelters for two $4^1/2$ inch (112 mm) guns, were installed together with barracks for 350 soldiers, a new jetty and a railway line to transport supplies around the island.

Gilfach Goch Industrial Trail, off B4564, $2^1/2$ miles (4 km) west of Tonyrefail (OS 170: SS 983895).

This 2 mile (3 km) long trail, starting at the site of the Six Bells Hotel, explores the industrial sites of this small coal-mining valley which was the setting for Richard Llewelyn's famous novel *How Green Was My Valley.*

Hengoed Viaduct.

Glamorganshire Canal, Merthyr Tydfil (OS 160: SO 047062) to Aberfan (OS 170: SO 070007).

In 1790 a bill for the construction of the Glamorganshire Canal, running from Merthyr Tydfil's ironworks to the port at Cardiff, was promoted by the ironmasters Crawshay, Guest and Homfray. The canal was constructed in the years 1792-4 and represented a tremendous achievement, involving much expensive cutting in a narrow winding valley with a drop of 543 feet (165 metres) and forty locks in a distance of 25 miles (40 km). The canal starts outside Chapel Row (see under Merthyr Tydfil: Cyfarthfa Ironworks). A 3³/₄ mile (6 km) dry stretch of the canal can be reached from the car park in front of Merthyr's technical college, via the tarmac road past the sports centre; the route goes under a three-arched bridge (built in 1850 to carry the Vale of Neath Railway) and then along the old towpath past Glandyrus House and some industrial cottages (dating back to 1820) at Abercanaid and on into open countryside, passing Troedyrhiw on the way, before arriving at Aberfan. A ³/₄ mile (1 km) water-filled stretch of the canal remains at **Whitchurch**, near Cardiff (OS 171: ST 143804); close by, at **Melingriffith** (OS 171: ST 142799), is a restored water pump, with an undershot waterwheel, built in 1807 to return water to the canal after feeding the nearby tinplate works (now gone).

Hengoed Viaduct, Hengoed (OS 171: ST 155949).

This splendid stone-built viaduct of fifteen arches was constructed across the Rhymney valley in 1857 for the Newport, Abergavenny and Hereford Railway. It is 850 feet (260 metres) long and was designed by Charles Liddell. Beneath the tall arches of the viaduct is a nineteenth-century flannel mill (privately owned) which is now used for storage.

Machen Forge Industrial Trail, Ty'n-y-coedcae, 2 miles (3 km) east of Caerphilly (OS 171: ST 195881). Telephone: Caerphilly Mountain Countryside Service, 0222 813356.

This trail starts at the Greenmeadow Inn and follows a disused tramroad past the shortlived ironworks at Ty'n-y-coedcae. It continues along lanes past the sites of two coal mines to a footpath alongside the Rhymney river and the site of Machen Forge and Tinplate Works. The forge, which had existed here since the sixteenth century, changed over to tinplate manufacture in 1826 and closed in 1886. Ruined stables near the disused viaduct are all that is left of the forge buildings.

Maesteg: Llynfi Ironworks, Llynfi Road (OS 170: SS 849918).

The Llynfi Ironworks was established by the Cambrian Iron and Smelter Company in 1837 and lasted until 1886. In 1839 the company built a fine blast-engine house which became known as the Cornstores; it has been converted to form the entrance to Maesteg Sports Centre. Remains of the blast-furnaces can be seen on the west side of the car park. At the bottom corner of the Llynfi Road car park is a cast iron bridge erected in 1835 to carry the parish road across the Afon Llynfi. A 'Maesteg Iron Trail' leaflet has been published by the Llynfi Valley Civic Society.

Merthyr Tydfil: Brecon Mountain Railway. See chapter 9.

Merthyr Tydfil: Cefn Viaduct, Cefncoed-ycymer (OS 160: SO 031078).

This is a strikingly tall and slim stone viaduct of fifteen arches, 120 feet (37 metres) high and built on a graceful curve across the Taf Fawr valley. It was erected in 1866 for the Brecon and Merthyr Railway to the designs of H. Conybeare and A. Sutherland, who were also responsible for the smaller viaduct for the same company across the Taf Fechan valley at Pontsarn (OS 160: SO 045099).

Merthyr Tydfil: Cyfarthfa Ironworks (OS 160: SO 037070).

The remains of the blast-furnaces and slag tips cover a vast area for this was in its heyday one of the most important and largest ironworks in southern Wales. The ironworks were started, slightly further upstream, in 1766. It was later acquired by Richard Crawshay of Yorkshire and by 1803 was the largest ironworks in Britain, employing 1500 men. **Pontycafnau** (SO 038071), a little to the north, spans the Afon Taf and was built in 1793 by Watkin George as a tramroad bridge which also served as an aqueduct to supply water to the ironworks. It is constructed of cast iron and has a box deck supported on A-frames. Within the original ironworks, but now divided from the furnaces by a road and industrial estate, an unusual octagonal chapel of ease was erected in 1803; only a few walls survive, but next to it stands **Chapel Row** (SO 044067), a short terrace of workers' cottages. The cottage (number 4) where the composer Joseph Parry was born in 1841 is open to visitors and has an exhibition devoted to the life of the composer. The Glamorganshire Canal (constructed in 1794) terminated just outside the cottages.

Merthyr Tydfil: Dowlais Ironworks, Dowlais (OS 160: SO 068076).

The Dowlais Ironworks was the earliest of the five ironworks which made Merthyr Tydfil the greatest ironmaking town in the world in the early nineteenth century. It was started in 1759, later taken over by John Guest and by the middle of the nineteenth century had eighteen blast-furnaces and employed over

Cefn Viaduct, Merthyr Tydfil.

seven thousand men, women and children, overtaking Cyfarthfa as the world's largest ironworks. The chief remains are the late nineteenth-century yellow and red brick **blast-engine house**, with its classical cast iron portico (on the south side of the A4102), and the handsome two-storey **stables** (at SO 067079) erected in 1820 by Sir John Guest. The first floor of the stables was used as a school for the workmen's children; the building has now been converted into houses.

Merthyr Tydfil: Penydarren Tramroad, Quakers Yard (OS 171: ST 906965).

The 9 mile (13 km) tramroad was built between Merthyr Tydfil and Abercynon between 1799 and 1802. Two years later, as a result of a bet between the ironmasters Richard Crawshay of Cyfarthfa and Samuel Homfray of Penydarren, it was the scene of Richard Trevithick's trials with the world's first steam locomotive to run successfully on rails. The engine hauled five trucks loaded with 10 tons of iron at a speed of 5 miles (8 km) an hour and won Homfray the thousand guineas' bet. The track of the tramroad can be followed for about 2 miles (3 km) from Quakers Yard as far as **Pontygwaith** where there is a fine eighteenth-century hump-backed bridge by William Edwards. At the Merthyr end the tramroad passed under the hillside in a tunnel, the entrance of which has been restored and can be seen just east of the A470 road (OS 170: SO 055048). A 'Taff Valley Trail' leaflet has been published by Merthyr Tydfil Groundwork Trust.

Merthyr Tydfil: Ynysfach Engine House, Ynysfach Road, Merthyr Tydfil CF48 1AG (OS 160: SO 045062). Telephone: 0685 721858.

The four-storey engine house was built in 1836 to serve the furnaces at the Ynysfach Ironworks, which were a subsidiary of the much larger Cyfarthfa Ironworks. The works started in 1801 with two furnaces; two more furnaces were added in 1836. The ironworks closed in 1874. The engine house is a plain but well built structure incorporating semi-circular arches typical of the Cyfarthfa style. The engine house is now the home of the Merthyr Tydfil Heritage Trust and after years of neglect it has been converted to a heritage centre of the iron and steel industry in Merthyr where life-sized displays and an audio-visual show set the scene.

Nash Point Lighthouse, Marcross (OS 170: SS 919680).

The Bristol Channel has the second highest tidal range in the world and consequently can be dangerous for navigation. Nash Point has been the scene of a number of shipwrecks and it was as the result of one of these in 1831, when the steamer *Frolic* ran aground on a nearby sandbank (with the loss of eighty passengers), that two lighthouses were erected 1000 feet (305 metres) apart and aligned so that when a ship was following the correct course only one of the lights would be visible. The west lighthouse is now disused and only its tower remains.

Neath and Tennant Canals, Maesgwyn (OS 170: SN 858051) to Tonna (SS 769988). Telephone: 0639 633531.

The Neath Canal was opened in 1795 and ran from Glyn Neath all the way down the Vale of Neath to the mouth of the river Neath near Briton Ferry. Work by the Neath and Tennant Canals Preservation Society has resulted in the restoration of a lock and has turned 4 miles (6 km) of the canal near Resolven (SN 826031) into a navigable waterway again. To the north-east, further stretches of the canal can be seen at Rheola, where a cast iron aqueduct carries a stream over the canal (SN 841040) and at Maesgwyn. To the south-west, at Aberdulais (SS 773993) a 340 foot (104 metre) long stone aqueduct carries the later Tennant Canal (built 1820-4) across the Neath to join the Neath Canal in a basin where there is a skew bridge known as Pont Gam ('crooked bridge'). The original workshops for the Neath Canal at Tonna (SS 769988) have been restored and now form part of the Tonna Conservation Area, which also includes a lock, lock house, forge and stables.

New Tredegar: Elliott Colliery Winding House (OS 171: SO 037027).

This very large stone-built winding house, erected in 1891, houses a twin tandem compound engine which once wound the cages up and down to the colliery working levels. Almost all traces of the colliery itself have gone following land reclamation. The winding house is currently being developed into a museum with exhibits devoted to the history of coal mining in the valley.

Pontrhydyfen: Pont Fawr Aqueduct (OS 170: SS 795941).

The massive four-arched aqueduct, 159 feet (140 metres) long by 75 feet (23 metres) high, which strides across the Afan valley, was built in 1824-7 by John Reynolds to supply water for his ironworks further down the valley. After 1841 it was used both by a railway and, apparently, by small boats. It is now used as a footpath. Half a mile (800 metres) to the west a ten-arched viaduct was built in 1897-8 to carry the South Wales Mineral Railway.

Pontypridd: Pont-y-ty-pridd or Hen Bont (OS 170: ST 074904).

This graceful bow-shaped stone bridge (its names mean 'bridge by the earthen house' and 'old bridge') was built across the Afon Taf in 1756 by the nonconformist minister and arch-itect William Edwards. With a clear span of 140 feet (44 metres), it was, at the time of its erection, the longest single-arch bridge in Britain. It was on the itinerary of every eight-eenth-century traveller in search of the pictur-esque. Success was not easily achieved and Edwards's earlier attempts to span the Taf, in 1746 and 1751, ended in failure. He suc-ceeded in overcoming the problems created by the bridge's weight by piercing the abutments with cylindrical holes, three on each side of diminishing size, thus reducing its weight and allowing a passage for floor waters. The bridge is now open for pedestrians only.

Port Eynon: The Salt House (OS 159: SS 469846).

The ruins of a sixteenth-century house and sea-salt works lie on a spur of rock jutting into the sea just east of Port Eynon Point. It had been almost completely buried beneath blown sand until excavated in 1986/7. Below the house, which was converted into two cottages in the eighteenth century, are two stone-lined

Pont Fawr Aqueduct, Pontrhydyfen.

reservoirs. Salt water was pumped from the lower reservoir to the higher, where it was heated to leave a residue of salt after evaporation.

Porth: Rhondda Heritage Park, Lewis Merthyr, Coed Cae Road, Trehafod CF37 7NP (OS 170: ST 040911). Telephone: 0443 682036.

At the peak of the coal-mining industry the two Rhondda valleys had almost fifty collieries. All have now closed, the last survivor, the Maerdy Colliery in the Rhondda Fach valley, shutting in December 1990. The Lewis Merthyr colliery, which was one of the most important in the Rhondda Fawr valley, closed in 1983; it was reopened in 1989 as the centre of an ambitious industrial heritage park. Its two winding towers, known as 'Trefor' and 'Bertie', together with their engine houses, now form the centrepiece of the heritage park. A multi-media exhibition, 'Black Gold', is set in the pithead buildings and tells the story of coal mining in the Rhondda, the most famous of all the Welsh mining valleys. There is also a visitor centre and there are riverside and forest walks nearby. Gradually a variety of buildings is being re-erected to recreate a typical Welsh mining village.

Rhymney: Butetown (Y Drenewydd) (OS 161: SO 104092).

This is an interesting example of estate planning in the 'classical' manner. It comprises three parallel symmetrical terraces with projecting end units and taller middle sections with wide overhanging eaves. It was built between 1802 and 1804 as a model community to house workers at the nearby ironworks (now gone) and is reputed to have been designed by the manager of the ironworks, R. Johnson. A fourth terrace was planned but never built.

Swansea: Equatorial Observatory, Penlle'r-gaer, near Gorseinon (OS 159: SN 622990).

This curious cylindrical observatory tower stands in the grounds of the Lliw Valley Borough Council's offices. It was built in 1846 by John Dillwyn-Llewelyn, whose varied interests included astronomy, photography and

Pont-y-ty-pridd, Pontypridd.

The Salt House, Port Eynon.

Rhondda Heritage Park, Porth.

botany. A single-storey laboratory made with specially designed hollow insulating bricks (shown at the Great Exhibition of 1851) stands in front of the tower. The observatory and tower were renovated in 1981.

Swansea: Morris Castle Industrial Housing, Morriston (OS 159: SS 659963).

Morriston was founded about 1768 by Sir John Morris to attract and house workers for his copper works. William Edwards was employed by Morris to lay out the new town on a

Scott's Pit, Swansea.

grid plan and also to design a new bridge (1780) and a chapel. Some time between 1768 and 1775 Morris also built the curious block of early industrial flats known as Morris Castle on a hill above the town. It was constructed of local sandstone with copper slag string-courses and was embellished with mock battlements. Only the remains of two gable walls now stand, but originally the quadrangular block comprised four-storey towers at each corner linked by three-storey wings around a central courtyard.

Swansea: Scott's Pit, Llansamlet (OS 170: SS 697983).

The tall three-storey engine house, built to accommodate a Cornish pumping engine, the foundations of two boilers and a 500 foot (150 metre) deep shaft (now capped with concrete) are the main surviving features of this colliery, which was sunk in 1817-19. The coal mine was not successful and was worked only until 1842, but the engine house was recommissioned in 1872 in order to drain the nearby Cae Pridd colliery.

Swansea Canal, Ynysmeudwy (OS 160: SN 740058).

This was the last of the major canals to be opened (1798) in southern Wales. It was 15 miles (24 km) long with 36 locks and linked the head of the Tawe valley with Swansea. It was closed to traffic in 1931 but a $1\frac{1}{2}$ mile (2 km) stretch between Ynysmeudwy and Pontardawe is still in water and offers pleasant walks along the towpath. At Ynysmeudwy a double lock and a canal lengthman's hut have been restored. Half a mile (800 metres) down the canal (at SN 737050) are remains of a branch canal with its own loading dock for transhipping coal from an inclined tramroad. Further up the canal at Ystalyfera (SN 772092) the canal is carried across the Afon Twrch by a three-arched masonry aqueduct.

9
Other places to visit

Brecon Mountain Railway, Pant, Merthyr Tydfil. Telephone: 0685 4854. 2 miles (3 km) north-east of Merthyr Tydfil.

This 2 mile (3 km) long narrow-gauge railway line follows the trackbed of the old Brecon and Merthyr Railway (opened 1866). Vintage steam locomotives haul passenger trains from Pant station through delightful upland scenery to the banks of the Taf Fechan reservoir and the foothills of the Brecon Beacons. There are a locomotive workshop, shop and cafe at Pant.

Claypits Pottery, Ewenny, Bridgend CF35 5AP. Telephone: 0656 661733. On B4265 1½ miles (2 km) south of Bridgend.

On the opposite side of the road to the Ewenny Pottery, Claypits Pottery produces a wide range of pots and ceramics in stoneware and porcelain. Gold and silver jewellery is also made here and the showroom is open to the public.

Ewenny Pottery, Ewenny, Bridgend CF35 5AP. Telephone: 0656 653020. On B4265 1½ miles (2 km) south of Bridgend.

The pottery is thought to have been founded in 1610 using clays found locally and is said to be the oldest in Wales. It makes traditional earthenware pottery and visitors are able to see the potter at work.

Model House Design and Craft Centre, Bull Ring, Llantrisant CF7 8EB. Telephone: 0443 237758.

The centre is housed in a three-storey nineteenth-century workhouse which has been completely transformed to provide a dozen light and airy craft studios. The studios are openly planned so that visitors can see the craftsmen and women at work. Appropriately, since Llantrisant is now the home of the Royal Mint, there is also an interesting exhibition with displays and exhibits relating to the history of coin production. Crafts produced in the centre can be bought in the gallery shop on the ground floor and there is a cafe on the top floor.

Old Mill Forge and Melin Ystrad, Ystrad Mynach. Telephone: 0443 812827. At side of A469 1 mile (1.6 km) south of Ystrad Mynach.

The blacksmith at the smithy makes wrought ironwork and still shoes horses and ponies. Nearby is Melin Ystrad, an eighteenth-century corn mill which was last used on a commercial basis in the 1880s. The L-shaped building has wide arches and is gradually being restored. It still retains its undershot waterwheel and millpond.

Old Wool Barn Craft Centre, Verity's Court, off High Street, Cowbridge.

This large stone building was formerly a barn for collecting shorn sheep fleeces and is approached from the High Street by a cobbled lane. It has now been converted into a fascinating working craft centre and studios for hand-weaving, porcelain, watercolour, graphic design and illustration, antique restoration and upholstery and other crafts.

Penscynor Wildlife Park, Cilfrew, Neath SA10 8LF. Telephone: 0639 642189. Off A465.

The park is set in 11 acres (4.5 ha) of trees, ponds and streams on the edge of the moorlands. There are 350 types of animals and birds, including colourful tropical birds, an aquarium with tropical fish, and penguins, sea-lions and monkeys. For the more adventurous there is an Alpine Slide from the hilltop. There are also a playground and a restaurant.

Plantasia Hothouse, Parc Tawe, Swansea SA1 2AL. Telephone: 0792 474555.

This is a hothouse with a difference. Within this giant glass pyramid situated near the city centre it is possible to stroll through three different climatic zones – each with its own distinctive plants – arranged at varying levels, and walk under a man-made waterfall. There are a thousand varieties of plants on show, including cacti, orchids and palms. There is also an aviary with exotic birds.

Stuart Crystal Glassworks, Angel Lane, Aberbargoed, near Bargoed. Telephone: 0443 820044.

Hand-made crystal glass has been made here since 1966. Self-conducted tours are available on weekdays only, when glass can be seen being blown and cut to intricate designs. Glass can be bought at the factory shop.

Brecon Mountain Railway, Merthyr Tydfil.

Plantasia Hothouse, Swansea.

Techniquest, 72 Bute Street, Pierhead, Cardiff CF1 6AA. Telephone: 0222 460211.

Although the purpose of this unusual attraction is to explore the world of science and technology and to bring it to life, one does not have to be scientifically minded to enjoy it. Visitors are encouraged to handle the exhibits to see how they work and to participate in solving the puzzles. There are holograms, mirrors, magnets, tricks with light and a puffing dragon, as well as imaginative experiments demonstrating the principles behind much of what we take for granted in everyday life.

Welsh Hawking Centre, Weycock Road, Barry CF6 9AA. Telephone: 0446 734687. On A226, 2 miles (3 km) north-west of Barry.

The centre has more than two hundred birds of prey, including eagles, falcons, hawks and owls. Many of the birds of prey are flown from the adjacent flying field, weather permitting, in the afternoons during the season. Other attractions include a children's animal park with rabbits, goats and donkeys and duck and fish ponds. Falconry courses are held from September to March.

10
Famous people

Thomas Bowdler (1754-1825)

Bowdler, the son of a wealthy and pious father, was born near Bath. He became a doctor of medicine as well as an enquiring traveller and an ardent, but critical, admirer of Shakespeare. It was for the latter attribute that he is chiefly remembered for during the last fourteen years of his life, which he spent in Swansea, he carefully edited the Bard's plays and brought out a ten-volume *Family Shakespeare* in which all 'words and expressions which are of such a nature as to raise a blush on the cheek of modesty' were erased. As a result of his censorious efforts the word *bowdlerise*, meaning 'to expurgate (from a book) words or passages considered indelicate or offensive' came into the English language. Bowdler is buried in Oystermouth churchyard.

The Bute family

In 1766 the already wealthy John, Lord Mountstuart (1744-1814), son and heir of the third Earl of Bute (who had been prime minister in 1762-3), became even richer by marriage to Charlotte Windsor, heiress of the Herbert and Windsor families. With the marriage came also possession of Cardiff Castle and estates in Cardiff and vast areas of mineral rights in the nearby valleys. He was created Baron Cardiff of Cardiff Castle in 1776 and in the following year he began alterations to the castle to make it more habitable. In 1796 he was created first Marquess of Bute.

The second Marquess (1793-1848) is generally regarded as 'the creator of modern Cardiff', which during his time grew rapidly from a small market town to become one of the most important ports in Wales. In 1814 he succeeded his grandfather as Marquess and came into possession of his valuable and widespread estates. In order to provide an outlet for the minerals, particularly coal, issuing from the estates he risked his fortune and built the Bute West Dock, between 1830 and 1839, at a cost of £350,000. It was the first in a series of docks which caused Cardiff to grow to become the world's most important coal-exporting port. The second Marquess was a generous patron of the arts and of the Anglican church and education, spending £35,000 on building churches in the area and founding national schools in Cardiff and Llantrisant.

The third Marquess (1847-1900) was also closely identified with the cultural and commercial life of Cardiff, becoming Mayor of Cardiff in 1890. During his life the Bute East Dock (1861) and the Roath Dock (1887) were built. A scholarly man, he was author and translator of a number of works. He was also responsible for carrying out excavations, restorations and some exotic rebuilding at both Cardiff Castle and Castell Coch.

During the time of the fourth Marquess (1881-1947) the Bute Docks were sold to the Great Western Railway and the family's mineral reserves were nationalised. The fifth Marquess (1907-56) gave Cardiff Castle and its park to the city in 1947.

Sir Thomas Button (died 1634)

The date of Thomas Button's birth is not known but he was probably brought up in a house on the site of the present Duffryn, near St Lythans. Button went to sea about 1589 and in 1612-13 commanded an expedition sent to search for Henry Hudson, who had been looking for a way to India via the north-west passage. Button did not find Hudson but explored a large part of Hudson Bay in what is now northern Canada. He was knighted on his return and became an admiral.

The Crawshay family

Richard Crawshay (1739-1810) was a Yorkshireman who, after making his fortune in London, bought out the leases of Cyfarthfa Ironworks near Merthyr Tydfil and eventually, in 1794, became the sole owner of the works. He was one of the chief promoters of the Glamorganshire Canal between Merthyr and Cardiff, which opened in 1794. Taking advantage of the boom in the iron trade as a result of the Napoleonic Wars, he expanded the ironworks and built new furnaces. He is buried at Llandaf.

Richard's only son, William Crawshay I (1764-1834), took little interest in the manufacture of iron but instead took charge of the company's selling agency in London. He died in Stoke Newington.

His son, William II (1788-1867), managed

both the Cyfarthfa and Hirwaun ironworks and bought up the Treforest ironworks. He expanded the works still further into an industrial giant, producing enormous quantities of iron and coal. Because of his tough attitude towards his employees, particularly at the time of the famous Merthyr Riots (1831), he became known as the 'Iron King'. He was responsible for the building of Cyfarthfa Castle in 1825. After buying Caversham Park, Berkshire, he left the running of the ironworks to his youngest son, Richard Thompson Crawshay (1817-79), who had been born at Cyfarthfa. The latter rebuilt Vaynor parish church and when he died he was buried in the churchyard there under a massive stone slab inscribed with the words GOD FORGIVE ME.

John Dillwyn-Llewelyn (1810-82)

Dillwyn-Llewelyn lived at Pen-lle'r-gaer, near Swansea. He inherited his father's scientific interests and was a keen botanist. He collaborated with Wheatstone in his electric telegraph experiments and with Fox Talbot in his photographic developments. In 1846 he built an observatory in the grounds of his house which still stands (see chapter 8).

William Edwards (1719-89)

Edwards, a farmer's son, was born at Groeswen, Eglwysilan, near Caerphilly. He became a stone-mason and at twenty he moved to Cardiff to build a small iron furnace. He also began preaching and in 1745 he became joint pastor of the Independent chapel at Groeswen, one of the earliest non-conformist chapels in Glamorgan. Edwards is best known, however, for the many bridges he built all over southern Wales. His graceful bridge at Pontypridd (see chapter 8) is deservedly famous. He was also responsible, c.1770, for the layout of Morriston, near Swansea, as a model town and for a chapel there in 1782. He is buried in Eglwysilan churchyard.

Sir Josiah Guest (1785-1852) and Lady Guest (1812-95)

Josiah John Guest, born at Dowlais, near Merthyr Tydfil, was descended from a line of Shropshire farmers. He inherited a share in the Dowlais Ironworks from his father and managed it in such a way that it soon became the largest and most productive ironworks in the

world. By 1849 he had become sole proprietor. He was concerned for the welfare of his workmen and established a school and library in Dowlais as well as building the church there. He was the first MP for Merthyr and was chief promoter of the Taff Vale Railway.

Lady Charlotte Guest, the wife of Sir Josiah and daughter of the Earl of Lindsey, is remembered as the translator (together with John Jones of Bala) of the medieval Welsh folk epic *The Mabinogion* into English between 1838 and 1849. She was a lifelong collector and published books on fans and playing cards. Lady Guest took an active part in promoting the welfare of the workmen and in 1863 had the Guest Memorial Library built in memory of her husband.

Julia Ann Hatton (1764-1838)

The poet and novelist Julia Hatton was born in Worcester. She was the seventh child of the strolling actors Roger Kemble and Sarah Ward; her sister was the actress Sarah Siddons. She married William Hatton and in 1799 they leased the Swansea Bathing House. After her husband's death in 1806 she moved to live in Kidwelly but in 1809 returned to settle in Swansea, where she devoted herself to writing and became known as 'Ann of Swansea'. She wrote two books of poetry, a dozen novels and a play.

Evan James (1809-78) and James James (1833-1902)

Evan James and his son James were the joint authors of the Welsh national anthem. Evan was a weaver living at Argoed in Gwent and it was here that James was born. The family then moved to Pontypridd and Evan, who wrote poetry in his spare time, took over a woollen factory there. In 1856, while living in Pontypridd, Evan wrote the words for 'Hen Wlad fy Nhadau' and James composed the air to go with it. The tune was later harmonised and the song soon became so popular that eventually it took its place as the national anthem.

Alun Lewis (1915-44)

The poet and short-story writer Alun Lewis was born at Cwmaman, near Aberdare, and after studying at Cowbridge School and in Aberystwyth taught for a brief period at Lewis'

School, Pengam. Despite pacifist leanings, he resigned his teaching post and enlisted in the Royal Engineers in 1940. He was commissioned in the infantry and went to India in 1943. He is judged by many to be one of the finest poets of the Second World War. He was killed in an accident in 1944 while in India. His book of poems, *Raider's Dawn*, and his book of short stories, *The Last Inspection*, were both published in 1942 while he was on active service. Three other books were published posthumously. There is a memorial to Lewis in Aberdare Library.

Griffith Morgan (1700-37)

The legendary cross-country runner Griffith Morgan, better known as Guto Nyth-brân, was born at Llanwynno, near Pontypridd. Many of the stories concerning him are probably fiction, but the last one, at least, appears to be true. According to this he dropped dead suddenly, at the age of 37 after running the 12 miles (19 km) between Newport and Bedwas church in the incredible time of 53 minutes. A cross-country race is held every New Year's Eve in Guto's honour.

Iolo Morgannwg. See Edward Williams.

Richard 'Beau' Nash (1674-1762)

Nash was Glamorgan's most notable figure in the world of fashion. He was born in Swansea of Pembrokeshire parents and was educated in Carmarthen. In 1705 he went to Bath and two years later was appointed its Master of Ceremonies. Known in Bath as 'Beau Nash', he controlled the manners and behaviour of visitors by his stern rule and made Bath one of the most elegant and fashionable resorts in eighteenth-century Europe. He was buried with much pomp in Bath Abbey.

Ivor Novello (1893-1951)

The composer Ivor Novello, son of Clara Novello-Davies (1861-1943), conductor of the famous Royal Welsh Ladies Choir, was born in Cardiff as David Ivor Davies. His first song was published when he was only fifteen and he later became an actor manager. He is remembered most of all for songs such as 'Keep the Home Fires Burning', which won him fame during the First World War, and 'We'll Gather Lilacs in the Spring'. As well as writing plays he also wrote musical comedies such as *Glamorous Night* and *King's Rhapsody*.

Guto Nyth-brân. See Griffith Morgan.

Joseph Parry (1841-1903)

Born in Merthyr Tydfil, the composer Parry was working as a collier boy by the age of nine and in 1854 emigrated to the United States with his family. He worked in Pennsylvania ironworks until 1865 and during his spare time studied music. After winning competitions at the National Eisteddfod, a public fund was opened to enable him to study at the Royal Academy of Music in London. He returned to

Statue of William Price (1800-93), Llantrisant.

the USA and opened a college of music at Danville before being appointed in 1874 first Professor of Music at the University College of Wales; he later taught at Cardiff and Swansea. He composed many musical works including 'Myfanwy', the hymn-tune 'Aberystwyth' and two operas. His childhood home, at 4 Chapel Row, Merthyr Tydfil, is open to visitors. He spent his last years in Penarth and is buried in the churchyard of St Augustine's church.

Richard Price (1723-91)

The radical philosopher and dissenting minister Richard Price was born at Tynton, Llangeinor, near Bridgend. On the death of his parents he went to live in London with his uncle and in 1744 he was appointed family chaplain to George Streatfield at Stoke Newington. At 36 he published *A Review of the Principal Questions and Difficulties in Morals*, a classic statement on ethics. In 1756 he was elected to the Royal Society. He was one of the earliest authorities on actuarial and life insurance matters, wrote on the National Debt and advised William Pitt in financial matters. He was an advocate of parliamentary reform and defended the colonists in the American War of Independence, but his best remembered work is *A Discourse on the Love of Our Country* (1789), in which he enthusiastically greeted the opening events of the French Revolution.

William Price (1800-93)

This eccentric man of many parts was born at Ty'n-y-coedcae, near Rudry in the Rhymney valley. Price practised as a doctor at Pontypridd and became well known as both a physician and a surgeon. He also claimed to be an archdruid and performed druidical rites at the Rocking Stone on Pontypridd Common dressed in a scarlet waistcoat, green cloth trousers and a fox-skin hat. He became notorious for his advocacy of free-love, Chartism, vegetarianism and cremation and for his hatred of vaccination, vivisection, orthodox religion, the ironmasters and the law. In 1838 Price began illegally building a druidical palace on land belonging to Lady Llanover at Glyntaf, but only the gateway towers were completed. A year later he fled to France dressed as a woman after the Chartist march on Newport. He was involved in many lawsuits, including a famous one in 1884 when he was accused of trying to burn the corpse of his infant son Iesu Grist (Jesus Christ). His acquittal resulted in the establishment in British law of the legality of cremation. At the age of 83 he took Gwenllian Llewelyn as his common-law wife and fathered her two children. He died at Llantrisant and was cremated at Caerlan Fields in accordance with his specific instructions.

John Prichard (1817-86)

The architect John Prichard was born at Llan-gan in the Vale of Glamorgan, where his father was rector. In 1847 he became diocesan architect of Llandaf and was responsible for the design of many churches and schools throughout the county as well as a number of houses and public buildings. He was also responsible for the restoration of Llandaf Cathedral between 1844 and 1857 and added the tower and spire at the south-west corner. Between 1852 and 1863 Prichard was in partnership with J. P. Seddon, one of the most original of the Victorian architects. Prichard was buried in the graveyard of Llandaf Cathedral.

Ceri Richards (1903-71)

The painter Ceri Richards was born at Dunvant, Swansea. He studied at the Swansea College of Art and although he lived in London for most of his later life he frequently returned to Swansea and often incorporated Gower features in his paintings. He was influenced by the work of Matisse but in 1936 became a member of the British Surrealist Group. Many of his paintings take inspiration from music and poetry and Richard's international reputation owes much to his series of paintings based on the poetry of Dylan Thomas.

Evan Roberts (1878-1951)

Roberts was born at Bwlchymynddd, near Gorseinon. He worked as a collier before training to become a Calvinistic Methodist minister. In 1904 he underwent an intense spiritual experience while preaching at Blaenannerch, near Newcastle Emlyn in Dyfed, and he became the focus of a religious awakening at his home chapel in Loughor. The religious revival spread rapidly to all parts of Wales and even to Liverpool, but during the winter of 1905-6 Roberts suffered a mental breakdown and enthusiasm for the revival quickly waned. Roberts was buried at Moriah Chapel, Loughor.

Dylan Thomas (1914-53)

Dylan Thomas, the best known of modern Welsh poets, was born in Swansea. He was educated at Swansea Grammar School, where his father taught English. His passion for poetry developed while at school. After leaving school he worked as a junior reporter on the *South Wales Daily Post* for just over a year and then devoted himself to writing poetry and short stories. He moved to London in 1934 and thereafter alternated between social life in the big city and periods of creative writing in Wales. Thomas married in 1937 and moved to live at Laugharne, Dyfed, the following year. Much of his earlier work is based on childhood memories of Swansea and holidays in the Carmarthenshire countryside. After periods living at Llan-gain, New Quay and Oxford, he returned to live in Laugharne in 1949. Thomas also wrote radio and film scripts, but his best known work is the 'play for voices', *Under Milk Wood.*

Edward Williams (1747-1826)

Better known by his bardic name of Iolo Morgannwg, Williams was born at Llancarfan in the Vale of Glamorgan. He worked as a stone-mason for most of his life but is remembered as a poet, writing in Welsh and English, and as a controversial antiquary. His first major work was a collection of poems which he attributed to Dafydd ap Gwilym but which were in fact by himself. He had a great influence on the Welsh literary and antiquarian scene in his day and claimed that the Welsh tradition could be traced directly back to the Druids. He was responsible for introducing the *Gorsedd* ceremony – an offspring of his fertile imagination – into the form of the eisteddfod. He died at Flemingston.

Cathays Park, Cardiff: aerial view.

11
Cardiff

No early closing day; provisions market week-days.

Although it is the capital of Wales and its largest city, Cardiff (Caerdydd) is a town of relatively recent development. At the beginning of the nineteenth century Cardiff was merely a quiet little market town, which had hardly changed since John Speed mapped it in 1610 and still retained its medieval street layout enclosed by town walls and overlooked by its castle. During the nineteenth century Cardiff grew at a phenomenal rate, following the opening of the Glamorganshire Canal in 1794 and the construction of the Taff Vale Railway in 1840, to become the greatest coal-exporting port in the world. After the First World War coal and iron exports waned but Cardiff continued to grow and emerged as the cultural, commercial and administrative capital of Wales. It was not, however, formally recognised as the principality's capital until a royal

decree was made in 1955. As Cardiff has grown so it has changed; yet, despite all the changes, it still retains its medieval street layout and though the town walls have long since been pulled down, the castle still overlooks the town.

Cardiff Castle (see chapters 3, 4 and 7) is the focal point of the city and its quadrangular Roman walls can be seen at the junction of Kingsway, Duke Street and pedestrianised Queen Street. Beyond the castle are the open spaces of Bute Park, landscaped by 'Capability' Brown in the eighteenth century, and the river Taff (Afon Taf). The nineteenth-century additions to the castle make a dramatic and picturesque backcloth to the park. Not far from the castle is the church of St John the Baptist (see chapter 5) with its splendid fifteenth-century Perpendicular tower. It stands at the heart of the city centre in what has now become a pedestrian precinct. The old Library

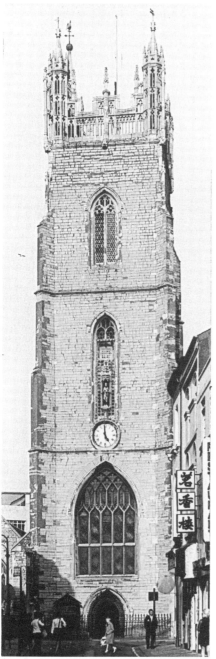

CHAPTER 11

Church of St John the Baptist, Cardiff.

(built in 1882), presently used as a craft centre, stands at the end of Trinity Street and opposite is St David's Hall, an excellent concert hall (built 1982) fitted in at the corner of the St David's Shopping Centre. Nearby, in The Hayes, is Tabernacle Chapel (see chapter 5).

Cardiff's shopping arcades are an interesting and practical feature of the city; there are more than a dozen, old and new, in the central area. Many of the nineteenth-century arcades off St Mary Street and High Street follow the historic lines of medieval burgage plots.

Apart from the city centre, Cardiff has three main areas of interest for visitors. These are the splendid civic centre in Cathays Park, the nineteenth-century commercial core in Butetown and the cathedral village of Llandaf.

The **civic centre** is a group of public and national buildings all built in white Portland stone and formally laid out around a small park. Together the buildings form a unique collection of architectural styles from the beginning of the twentieth century to the 1980s. They lie just north of the castle and town centre and can be approached from either Kingsway, The Friary (via an underpass) or Park Place. The three principal buildings, lying on the southern side facing the town, are the City Hall (built in 1904), in the centre, the National Museum of Wales (see chapter 7) and the Law Courts (built 1904). The City Hall, with its domed council chamber and flamboyant clocktower, is worth exploring inside to see the Marble Hall lined with historical statues and the richly decorated Assembly Hall. In the Gorsedd Gardens in front of the National Museum are a statue of David Lloyd George (1863-1945) and a druidical circle (the Gorsedd Circle) of standing stones erected for the 1905 National Eisteddfod. Behind the first row of buildings are the diminutive University of Wales Registry (built 1904), the graceful Glamorgan County Hall (built 1908) and the neo-classical Temple of Peace (built 1938) on the western side, the University College of Cardiff (various buildings from 1909 onwards) on the eastern side and the Welsh Office (built 1938 and 1980) on the northern side. The Welsh National War Memorial, an elegant temple-like building in the form of a circular colonnade (built in 1924), stands in the place of honour at the centre of the central park.

Butetown lies in the narrow wedge of land between the site of the Glamorganshire Canal and the docks (constructed between 1839 and 1907), to the south of the city centre; it was the scene of Cardiff's early industrial and commercial development. Bute Street leads straight as an arrow from the city centre to Butetown and was, for part of the nineteenth century, a fashionable area and the main business centre. St Mary's church (see chapter 5), an early example of the Romanesque revival, stands at the town end of Bute Street. At the seaward end of Bute Street is the Welsh Industrial and Maritime Museum (see chapter 7). A pleasant footpath overlooks the harbour and connects the component parts of the museum with a partially filled-in dock basin and the Pierhead Building (built 1896), an imposing landmark with pinnacled turrets and castellated clock-tower. Hidden away in Mount Stuart Square is the boldly pompous Coal Exchange (built 1885), once the nerve-centre of Cardiff and its docks. Nearby is the Bute Road Station, now housing the Railway Gallery (see chapter 7), the oldest station in Wales. The new South Glamorgan County Hall (built 1989) overlooks the Bute East Dock (opened 1855), which has been transformed into a boating lake as part of a vast scheme for redeveloping the Cardiff Bay area.

Llandaf was originally a lordship in its own right and a chartered borough, with its own market and fair; it did not officially become part of Cardiff until 1922. It is possible to walk all the way from Cardiff Castle to Llandaf Cathedral, 2 miles (3 km) to the north-west, along the banks of the Taff river, firstly through Bute Park and then, after crossing a footbridge near Blackweir, through Pontcanna Fields. The cathedral (see chapter 5) is built on one of the earliest church sites in Britain, in a hollow between the river and the village. On the hill above the cathedral is the Green, an informal open space surrounded by houses of various ages which gives Llandaf much of its 'village' character. The City Cross, traditionally the place where Archbishop Baldwin (accompanied by Gerald of Wales) preached the Third Crusade in 1188, stands near the centre and nearby are the craggy ruins of a thirteenth-century bell-tower. The twin-towered gate-house of the thirteenth-century Bishop's Castle (see chapter 4) stands at the end of the Green and behind it is the Cathedral School (built 1746), a three-storeyed Georgian building that was once the Bishop's Palace. St Michael's College (built 1880), with its modern chapel (1959) set in the middle of a grassy courtyard, and the Probate Registry (built 1857), a fine example of Victorian architecture, are both in

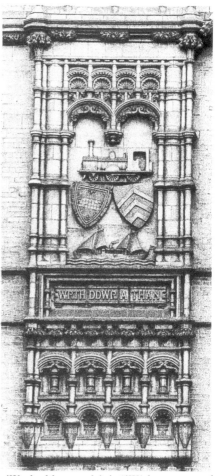

'Wrth ddwr a thân' ('With water and fire'), plaque on the Pierhead Building.

Cardiff Road.

Roath Park, 1¹/₄ miles (2 km) north of the city centre, is a linear park stretching northwards for 1¹/₂ miles (2.5 km). It includes playing fields, botanical gardens and a popular boating lake. The lighthouse at the southern end of the lake commemorates Captain Scott's ill-fated expedition to the South Pole in 1912 after leaving from Cardiff in the *Terra Nova*.

Coach tours

Guided coach tours of the city leave every hour from the Wales Tourist Board in Bridge Street on weekdays in the summer.

Cowbridge: High Street and Town Hall.

12
Towns and villages

ABERDARE (Aberdâr)
Early closing Thursday; market days Tuesday and Saturday.

During the nineteenth century Aberdare was one of the most important towns in Wales and vied with Merthyr Tydfil for pre-eminence amongst the valley towns. It lies near the head of the Afon Cynon in a bowl between gentle mountain slopes and, like Merthyr Tydfil, originally developed as an ironmaking town. The earliest ironworks, at Llwydcoed, were founded in 1800 by the Scales family and were soon followed by the Abernant Ironworks, founded in 1802 by the Homfrays, and the Gadlys Ironworks, founded in 1827 by Thomas Wayne. With the decline of the town's iron industry best-quality steam coal became the chief source of employment. Most of the collieries were sited in side valleys and had little effect on the town's appearance, which is more that of a market town than an industrial conglomeration. Virtually all evidence of Aberdare's earlier industries has, in any case,

disappeared and some of the industrial sites have been transformed into the Dare Valley Country Park (see chapters 2 and 8).

The long low lines of the medieval church of St John in its tree-lined churchyard adds to the illusion of Aberdare's non-industrial centre. Although founded as far back as the late twelfth century St John's was for centuries a chapelry of Llantrisant and did not obtain its own vicar until 1846. During the mid nineteenth century three new Anglican churches were built within ten years; one of these, St Elvan (1852), has a tall needle-like spire and makes a fine landmark in the centre of the town. There are also some good chapels, notably Bethania (1853), Siloa (1855) and the English Wesleyan (1859). In the nineteenth century Aberdare was noted for the high standard of its cultural life and in particular for its famous choir, *Côr Caradog*. The conductor of the choir, Griffith Rhys Jones, affectionately known as Caradog, took the specially formed 456-strong choir to compete at the Crystal Palace, London, where they

66

won the chief choral prize in 1872 and 1873. A bronze statue of the conductor, by William Goscombe John, stands in front of the seventeenth-century Black Lion Inn in Victoria Square. Aberdare was also the birthplace of the poet and short-story writer Alun Lewis (see chapter 10).

BARGOED

Bargoed developed as a mining town after 1886 when coal mines were sunk on Cefn Brithdir and at the side of the Rhymney river near its confluence with the Afon Bargoed. Before that date the whole area was given over to hill farming. Mining has ceased but glass is now made at Aberbargoed (see chapter 9). St Gwladys church is a mid nineteenth-century structure; it replaced the original Capel Gwladys, which was sited on Gelligaer Common. Another ancient chapel, Capel Brithdir, stood 2 miles (3 km) north of the town on Cefn Brithdir. Its position is marked by a concrete pillar where an early seventh-century inscribed stone and an early Christian cross slab were found. The seven-arched railway viaduct dates from 1858.

BARRY (Y Barri)
Early closing Wednesday.

The port and seaside resort of Barry developed from almost nothing during the latter part of the nineteenth century when Cardiff was unable to handle all of the continually increasing volume of coal being brought down from the valleys for export. It grew to prominence when the newly formed Barry Railway Company constructed a 73 acre (29 ha) dock amongst the saltmarshes between the little hamlet and Barry Island. When the dock was opened in 1889 it was said to be the largest dock in the world. The impressive Port Building (designed by Arthur E. Bell, 1898, in Portland stone and red brick) standing in front of the main dock is a neo-classical structure suggestive of civic pomp rather than commercial pride. Barry's Town Hall (1908) is similar in style but less grand.

A thirteenth- or fourteenth-century gateway and a few walls are all that remain of Barry Castle in Park Road; it was probably erected by the de Barri family but has no recorded history. Park Road leads to Porthkerry Country Park (see chapter 2) on the outskirts of the town, where a pleasant valley opens out on to a storm-washed pebble beach. Cold Knap Point was developed in 1926 for recreational

purposes with a swimming pool and boating lake. Nearby, at Glan-y-Mor, are remains of a Roman domestic building (see chapter 3).

Barry Island has a large sandy beach at Whitmore Bay which attracts thousands of holidaymakers. The island is connected to the mainland by a causeway which was built when Barry Dock was constructed between the island and the mainland. The crescent-shaped island was originally the home of the seventh-century St Baruch, who is reputed to be buried there. Development of the island as a resort started in 1905 with two terraces of stone bathing cubicles; it gathered momentum after the First World War, when the sea wall and promenade were constructed in 1922. Two years later Collin's fairground was opened and in 1966 Butlin's holiday camp was built on the island.

BRIDGEND (Pen-y-bont ar Ogwr)
Early closing Wednesday; market day Saturday.

Bridgend is a flourishing market town in the Vale of Glamorgan midway between Cardiff and Swansea. It is divided by the Ogwr river into Oldcastle on the east bank and Newcastle on the west bank. Nothing now remains of the old castle. St Mary's church (started 1885) with its elegant spire (added 1898) and the old police station in Court Road are the most interesting buildings in the older part of the town; both were designed by John Prichard. Oldcastle and Newcastle are connected by two bridges. The concrete road bridge was erected in 1912 to replace the 'new' bridge of 1821. The footbridge alongside dates from the fifteenth century although it was partly rebuilt in 1775 after flooding had demolished two of its arches.

The new castle (see chapter 4) itself stands opposite the town centre on a steep hill high above the Ogwr and dates from the twelfth century. At the foot of the hill is the Old Meeting House built in 1795 (see chapter 5). The parish church of St Illtud is medieval but its west tower was largely rebuilt in the mid nineteenth century, when the north aisle was added.

CAERPHILLY (Caerffili)
Early closing Wednesday; indoor market weekdays.

This former coal-mining town is situated at the lower end of the Rhymney valley and on the northern side of a steep ridge separating the coal-mining areas from the coastal plain. It was one of Glamorgan's medieval boroughs, but, apart from its enormous castle (see chapter 4), there is little to remind the visitor of its pre-industrial history. At the north-western corner of the castle the Romans built a fort about AD 75, strategically placed halfway between their other forts at Cardiff and Gelligaer.

Two nearby chapels are important in the history of Welsh nonconformity. Capel Groes-wen (3 km) west of the town, was the first Methodist chapel in Wales when it was built in 1742. William Edwards, the famous bridge-builder (see chapter 10), was pastor at Groes-wen from 1745 to 1789. Just to the south is Watford, built four years earlier as an Independent chapel. It was at Watford that the first synod of the Welsh Calvinistic Methodist Church, now known as the Presbyterian Church of Wales, was held in 1743.

The origin of Caerphilly cheese is obscure. Cheese has been produced on Glamorgan farms for centuries and presumably it was called Caerphilly cheese because most of it was sold at Caerphilly's cheese market. It was not until the end of the nineteenth century that it became well known and by then $2^1/2$ tons a week were being sold in the market. It was especially popular with colliers and, eaten together with bread, it became their staple diet underground.

CARDIFF (Caerdydd)
See chapter 11.

COWBRIDGE (Y Bont-faen)
Early closing Wednesday.

Cowbridge was once the chief market and most important town in the Vale of Glamorgan. Although little more than a single, but long and tightly packed, street on the line of a Roman road the town has considerable charm and is now happily bypassed by through traffic. It received its first borough charter in 1254. Medieval Cowbridge was a walled town which depended, at first, on St Quintin's Castle at Llanbleddian. Porth Melin, the southern gate of the town, still remains (see chapter 4). Next to the gate stands the Grammar School, founded in 1608 by Sir John Stradling of St Donat's. Later the school's patron was Jesus College, Oxford, which commissioned John Prichard to rebuild it in Tudor style. Nearby is the parish church of the Holy Cross (see chapter 5) with its curious octagonal tower.

Cowbridge still retains a number of seventeenth- and eighteenth-century town houses, such as Great House and Old Hall, and coaching inns, such as the Eagle Academy, in High Street. The Town Hall was built in 1806 as a house of correction and converted to its present form in 1832; there is an exhibition of local history in the former cells. There are two early nonconformist chapels: The Limes, built in 1825, and Ramoth (see chapter 5), built in 1828. Edward Williams, the eighteenth-century antiquary, better known as Iolo Morgannwg (see chapter 10), kept a bookshop at 14 High Street. Cowbridge was also the home of Glamorgan's first printing press, set up here in 1770 by Rhys Thomas of Llandovery.

GELLIGAER
This sprawling village at the lower end of the moorland ridge between the Rhymney and Taff valleys has a number of antiquities in the neighbourhood. Almost next to St Catwg's church are remains of two Roman forts buried beneath mounds of earth. The earlier fort was built of earth and timber while the later fort, dating from the early second century AD, was built in stone and had four gateways. $1^1/2$ miles (2 km) north are remains of five Roman practice camps. Further north again, on the summit of Gelligaer Common, is Carn Bugail burial chamber (see chapter 3).

KENFIG (Cynffig)
The parish of Kenfig is largely covered in sand. It was one of the 'rotten boroughs' and returned a member to Parliament until its corporation was abolished in 1883. In 1281 there were 142 burgages in the borough, but by 1572 there were only three burgages left. There are scant remains of a castle (see chapter 4) but almost everything else has been buried beneath the sands. The sixteenth-century town hall has been incorporated in the Prince of Wales public house. About 1250 a new church, St Mary Magdalene, was built on higher ground south-east of the old borough. The village of Mawdlam derives its name from the church. Inside the church there is a fine Norman font. Just inland from Sker Point are the ruined remains of Sker House, a medieval mansion altered in the sixteenth century and the setting for R. D. Blackmore's novel *The Maid of Sker*.

LLANCARFAN
This attractive village, lying in a small valley in the Vale of Glamorgan, has a stream

running through the middle of it. During the dark ages Llancarfan was associated with a monastic college founded by Catwg (or Cadog), a famous Celtic scholar, but apart from a late ninth-century pillar cross there is nothing now to remind the visitor of the village's earlier fame. There is a disproportionately large church (see chapter 5). Castle Ditches is an iron age hillfort to the east of the village. Edward Williams (see chapter 10), the eighteenth-century antiquary, was born at Pen-onn farm just south of the village.

LLANTRISANT

Early closing Thursday; market day Saturday.

The town is situated on a saddle between two hills and is approached by a steep road which winds up to the Bull Ring at the centre. Llantrisant was formerly a borough in its own right but the corporation was dissolved in 1883. The town still retains much of its earlier character. In the centre of the Bull Ring there is a statue of the eccentric Dr William Price (see chapter 10). Facing on to the Bull Ring is the Model Design and Craft Centre (see chapter 9), while just opposite and squeezed into a narrow frontage is Traditional Toys, a delightful shop with a nostalgic air of childhood. From the Bull Ring narrow streets, stone-paved lanes and footpaths lead to different parts of the old borough. An interesting circular walk goes up George Street to the Victorian police station (built 1876) and then turns sharp left past the modest little Town Hall (rebuilt 1773) – still used for meetings of the Court Leet in summer – and into a small park surrounding the fragmentary remains of Llantrisant Castle (not open). Follow the lane westwards and cross Yr Allt, a cobbled lane, to the stoutly built parish church (see chapter 5), and then go through the churchyard and into Swan Street. At the upper end of Swan Street cross back into Yr Allt and George Street, passing on the way the Gothic Parish Office of 1873.

The castle was built in a dominating position overlooking the northern part of the Vale of Glamorgan. It was while on his way to Llantrisant Castle that Edward II, after having fled to Wales in 1326, was betrayed. He was captured by Henry of Lancaster at Pant-y-Brad, just north of Llantrisant, and was held for a night in the castle before being taken back to England. Little remains of the castle now apart from fragments of a curtain wall and part of a thirteenth-century tower known as Twr-y-Gigfran (Raven Tower).

In 1968 a new Royal Mint was built at the Llantrisant Business Park just north of the town. Production was progressively transferred from Tower Hill, London, to the new mint so that by 1976 all coinage was being produced at Llantrisant.

LLANTWIT MAJOR (Llanilltud Fawr)

Early closing Wednesday.

Llantwit Major was once the site of the famous fifth-century monastery of St Illtud. During the dark ages it became renowned as a centre of learning and also as a mission centre for founding new churches. Nothing, however, remains to show where the monastery was sited or what it looked like. Traditionally it is said that it lay just north of the present church of St Illtud (see chapter 5). More is known of the Roman villa which was built north-west of the town although that too is now buried. The villa was excavated in 1888 and painted walls and elaborate mosaic floors were discovered but all were covered up again.

Although Llantwit Major has grown considerably in recent years, because of its nearness to the RAF airfield at St Athan, it still retains the attractive narrow winding streets and lanes and many fine buildings which give the town its historic character. The buildings include an interesting two-storey town hall, rebuilt in the sixteenth century on medieval foundations, a thirteenth-century gatehouse which once belonged to the monastery grange, a medieval circular dovecote near the church and a number of sixteenth-century houses and inns. The ruin known as Llantwit Major Castle, or the Old Place, was a sixteenth-century mansion.

A mile (1.6 km) south of Llantwit Major, the little Afon Col-huw runs down to a good beach. On either side the land rises up to rocky limestone cliffs. Nearby are the multiple ditches and ramparts of an iron age promontory fort known as Castle Ditches. Further along the coast is Summerhouse Point, with another promontory fort (see chapter 3).

LOUGHOR (Casllwchwr)

The town is of some antiquity and was a borough until 1886. An auxiliary fort known as *Leucarum* was built by the Romans, probably about AD 75, at Loughor to command the river crossing at the neck of the Gower peninsula. Most of the surface remains of the fort were destroyed when the South Wales Railway was built in 1852. In the middle ages the Normans erected a castle (see chapter 4) on the hill above the crossing point and within an angle of the fort. During the twentieth century Loughor has expanded eastwards to include the industrial township of **Gorseinon**. Evan Roberts, the famous revivalist preacher, was born at Bwlchymynydd (see chapter 10).

MAESTEG

Maesteg developed as an ironmaking and coal-mining town at the upper end of the Llynfi valley. The establishment of the ironworks in 1826 led to the construction of the Dyffryn Llynfi Railway (actually a tramroad) in 1828 to Porthcawl. A spelter works was later built at Caerau north of the town and a tinplate works to the south at Llwydarth. The dignified blast-engine house, known as the Cornstores, built in 1839 for the Llynfi Ironworks (see chapter 8) at Cwm-du, is the last relic of the iron industry. The large and rather garish Town Hall (designed by Henry C. Harris in 1881) dominates the centre of the town; it houses a public market on the ground floor and a large hall above with several paintings by Christopher Williams (1873-1934).

MERTHYR MAWR

Early closing Thursday.

This picturesque estate village is approached across a medieval bridge which retains its holes for sheep-dipping. The casually placed thatched cottages exude an air of peace and contentment and hardly anything seems to have changed since the pretty little church (see chapter 5) was rebuilt in 1849. A suspension bridge crosses the Ogmore river where a footpath leads to stepping stones giving access across the Ewenny river to Ogmore Castle (see chapter 4) on the other side. A mile (1.6 km) beyond the village are the fragmentary remains of Candleston Castle (see chapter 4) rising up from the sand dunes of Merthyr Mawr Warren (see Glamorgan Heritage Coast, chapter 2).

MERTHYR TYDFIL (Merthyr Tudful)

Early closing Thursday; market days Tuesday, Wednesday, Thursday and Saturday.

Merthyr Tydfil, 'capital' of the valleys, is situated at the upper end of the Taf valley on the northern edge of the coalfield and within sight of the Brecon Beacons. Until 1870 it was the largest and most important town in Wales. Its rapid expansion at the end of the eighteenth century and beginning of the nineteenth was

the result of industrial development which had first started as far back as the sixteenth century and had been brought to fruition by the demand for munitions during the American Civil War and the opening of the Glamorganshire Canal (see chapter 8) in 1794. By 1801 there were five ironworks scattered along the banks of the Afon Taf and its tributary at Dowlais, Plymouth, Cyfarthfa, Penydarren and Ynysfach. During the nineteenth century Merthyr was in the vanguard of industrial development and political radicalism. It was here that the world's first steam locomotive ran on the Penydarren Tramroad (see chapter 8) in 1804. There was considerable industrial unrest in 1816 and bloody riots in 1831. Following the latter Merthyr obtained representation in Parliament; its members have included the pacifist Henry Richard of Tregaron (1868-88) and Keir Hardie (1900-15), the first socialist MP.

The Romans built a fort just north of the town centre at Penydarren at the end of the first century AD but nothing is now visible. On the northern outskirts of Merthyr there are remains of Morlais Castle (see chapter 4), dramatically sited above the Taf Fach river. The earliest building in the town itself is the Court House, in Court Street, which dates from 1717. Much of the centre of Merthyr has been rebuilt since the Second World War and a shopping plaza stands on the site of the old market. Nearby are St Tudful's church (see chapter 5) and a delightful cast iron fountain canopy erected to commemorate the work of Lucy and Robert Thomas, pioneers of the steam-coal trade. In the High Street the elaborate terracotta-clad Town Hall of 1896 has been converted to new uses. The Miners' Hall in Church Street was built as a chapel, reputedly designed by the railway engineer Isambard Brunel, to take the place of an earlier chapel which stood on the site of the railway station built in 1853.

At the beginning of the nineteenth century the Cyfarthfa Ironworks (see chapter 8) was the largest in Britain. Cyfarthfa Castle (see chapter 6), once the home of the Crawshay family (see chapter 10), ironmasters of Cyfarthfa, stands in a park overlooking the ruins of the ironworks. Below the remains of the ironworks is Chapel Row, where the composer Joseph Parry (see chapter 10) was born in 1841. By the middle of the nineteenth century it was the Dowlais Ironworks (see chapter 8), north-east of the town centre, which

Penarth: the pier, promenade and gardens.

claimed to be the largest in the world. Little remains of the ironworks apart from the blast-engine house and the handsome Dowlais Stables. The imposing Guest Memorial Library (now a recreation centre) on the main road was designed by Sir Charles Barry in 1863 as a memorial to Sir John Guest (see chapter 10), commissioned by his wife. The Brecon Mountain Railway (see chapter 9) starts at Pant station nearby.

MOUNTAIN ASH (Aberpennar)

Mountain Ash developed as a mining town in the mid nineteenth century at the lower end of the Cynon valley after Deep Duffryn Colliery had been sunk in 1842. Dyffryn House (now a school) was the home of Lord Aberdare, the first Vice-chancellor of the University of Wales. At the summit of Twyn Brynbychan on the eastern side of the valley there is a

bronze age ring cairn with a central chamber. A seventh- to ninth-century pillar cross which once stood nearby is now in the National Museum of Wales.

NEATH (Castell Nedd)
Market day Wednesday.

Neath is an industrial and market town with a long history. Although it was long known as the site of the Roman *Nidum*, the location of the Roman fort (see chapter 3) was not discovered until 1949 when a housing estate was built near Neath Abbey Road. Adjoining the town centre are remains of Neath Castle (see chapter 4). The town developed around the castle and received its first charter in 1280. Neath and its surroundings were one of the earliest industrial centres in Glamorgan. Copper smelting started at nearby Aberdulais (see chapter 8) in the sixteenth century and Neath

71

continued to be the main centre of the industry until overtaken by Swansea in the eighteenth century. Part of the Neath Canal, which was opened in 1795, has been restored near the castle.

The parish church of St Thomas dates from the twelfth or thirteenth century and contains a tenth-century Celtic cross slab. The nineteenth-century church of St David (see chapter 5) is a prominent landmark. Gnoll House, an eighteenth-century mansion (now demolished) in a large park, was the home of Sir Humphrey Mackworth, one of the founders of the copper-smelting industry in Neath. The extensive ruins of Neath Abbey (see chapter 4), blackened by a century and a half of industrial pollution, lie a mile (1.6 km) to the west between the railway and the Neath Canal. Nearby are two enormous blast-furnaces belonging to the Neath Abbey Ironworks, established in 1792 by Quakers from Cornwall.

PENARTH
Early closing Wednesday.

In the mid nineteenth century Penarth was an isolated and straggling little village with a tiny gable-towered church on the headland overlooking the sea. The church was, despite its diminutive size, a landmark for sailors and when a dock was constructed in 1859 and a town and port developed it was decided to rebuild St Augustine's church (see chapter 5) with the same type of gable tower in order to conform to the existing Admiralty charts. The dock has closed to shipping and has been converted to a marina. Nearby is the pompous-looking Custom House.

The seaside town developed south of the headland, away from the dock area. Soon Penarth became a favourite place for shipowners and mine-owners to live, to the extent that at one time it was reputed that there were ten millionaires living in the town. A long promenade, with terraced gardens along one side, was constructed along the waterfront and a pier was built in 1894 at one end. Alexandra Park links the promenade to the town centre and at the side of the park a footpath winds its way up The Dingle to the Turner House Art Gallery (see chapter 7) in Plymouth Road.

A fine cliff walk links Penarth with **Lavernock** to the south. A small church, rebuilt in 1852, stands on Lavernock Point. It was on this headland on 11th May 1897 that Guglielmo Marconi received the first ever radio message across water, from the island of Flat Holm. The historic message was brief and to the point, simply asking 'Are you ready?'

PONTYPRIDD
Early closing Thursday; market days Wednesday and Saturday.

This lively market and industrial town stands at the confluence of the Taf and Rhondda rivers. Because of its situation the town became the natural focus of all coal and iron traffic coming down from the two Rhondda valleys and from the Cynon and Taf valleys on their way to the ports at Cardiff and Barry. The railway station, with the longest platform in Wales, was in its heyday one of the busiest stations in the principality. Little coal or iron comes down the valleys now but Pontypridd's open-air street market still flourishes.

Pontypridd: shoppers at the busy open-air market.

The town's name comes from the famous bridge erected across the Taf in 1756 (see chapter 8); it was earlier known as Newbridge. Next to the bridge is the Pontypridd Historical and Cultural centre (see chapter 5) in a converted chapel. During the nineteenth century Pontypridd was the home of Evan James and his son James James (see chapter 10), composers of the Welsh national anthem, *Hen Wlad fy Nhadau*. A fine memorial to the father and son stands in Ynysangharad Park near the old bridge. A pair of circular towers, known as Druid Towers, erected in 1838 in Craig-yr-Helfa Road on the opposite side of the valley at Glyn-taf, are all that was built of an intended eight-storey druidic palace and museum by the eccentric Dr William Price (see chapter 10). At Rhydfelin there are remains of the Treforest Tinplate works founded by William Crawshay in 1835.

PORT EYNON

This small village, originally a port, on the south coast of the Gower peninsula has a fine sandy beach and some dramatic cliff scenery. St Catwg's church was largely rebuilt in the 1860s. Near the churchyard is a lifelike memorial to the lifeboat crew who were drowned in 1916 while trying to rescue a ship in distress. The old lifeboat house is now a youth hostel. On the coastline between the village and Port Eynon Point are the remains of the sixteenth-century Salt House (see chapter 8). Just the other side of Port Eynon Point is a natural cave known as Culver Hole which has been closed off with a wall; according to local legend it was a favourite haunt for smugglers, but it may have been altered to form a dovecote.

PORTHCAWL

Early closing Wednesday.

Although Porthcawl is now a popular seaside resort it was developed in the nineteenth century as a port for coal and iron brought down from the valleys north of Bridgend. A horse-drawn tramroad was constructed from Maesteg to Porthcawl in the 1820s and a quay and dock were built in 1866. As a port it never quite achieved the hopes of its developers; the dock closed in 1907 and has now been filled in to form a car park, but the little harbour and quay at the end of the Esplanade still remain. The old police station in John Street is now a museum (see chapter 7). East of the harbour are two fine beaches, Sandy Bay and Trecco Bay, and behind these, where once there were

sand dunes, are the giant Coney Beach funfair and an immense caravan park. Rest Bay on the west side of the town is more rocky and remains largely unspoilt.

The fifteenth-century parish church at **Newton** has a massive west tower with a saddleback roof. On the far side of the green at Newton is St John's Well, otherwise known as Sandford's Well, which fills with water depending on the state of the tide $1/4$ mile (400 metres) away.

PORT TALBOT

Early closing Thursday; market days Tuesday and Saturday.

The industrial town and port developed in the nineteenth century around the village of Aberafan on a narrow strand between the steep bare hills and Swansea Bay. The name Port Talbot was given in 1836 in honour of the Talbot family of Margam Abbey (see chapter 6), when the old harbour was improved. The town developed rapidly after the construction of new docks in 1898. More recently a large deep-water harbour with a mile-long (1.6 km) breakwater has been formed to serve the vast Abbey Steelworks built just after the Second World War. St Mary's church was rebuilt on the site of the medieval parish church in 1859. St Catherine's church, Baglan, the abbey church of Margam and Beulah Chapel (see chapter 5 for all three) in the vicinity are worth visiting. West of the harbour entrance are 2 mile (3 km) long Aberafan Sands, backed by a promenade with a funfair and the Afan Lido. The Sandfields Estate behind the promenade is a large housing development built on former sand dunes.

RHONDDA

Rhondda – the most famous of all the coal-mining valleys – is in fact two valleys. The Rhondda Fawr (great) and the Rhondda Fach (little) run parallel courses through the mountains until they meet at Porth to the north-west of Pontypridd. Apart from a few isolated farms there had been no real settlement of these valleys before the development of coal mining there in the second half of the nineteenth century so that Thomas Roscoe could describe the area in 1836 as 'wild and mountainous where nature seemed to reign in stern and unbroken silence amidst her own eternal rocks.' Even today the mountains, forests and craggy cliffs are never far away. Blaenrhondda, in particular, lies in the midst of some of the

Rhondda: mountainous scenery at Blaenrhondda.

most dramatic and magnificent mountain scenery in southern Wales. Nearby a road, built by unemployed miners in the 1930s, heads from Treherbert for the pass at the end of the Rhondda Fawr valley, where, near the summit of Craig-y-llyn (see chapter 2), there are panoramic views across to the Brecon Beacons.

The opening of the coal mines brought great changes to the area and by the end of the nineteenth century both valleys had been completely built up. Within a space of forty years the population soared from 4000 to about 115,000 and continued to rise until the Depression of the 1930s. In the deeply etched valleys land was at a premium and housing was built in the form of long lines of terraces clinging to the valley sides, punctuated by nearly fifty collieries and more than 150 chapels. Now all the collieries have stopped working and many of the chapels have closed or been converted to other uses. The Lewis Merthyr colliery at Porth has become the centrepiece of the ambitious Rhondda Heritage Park (see chapter 8). Of the religious buildings the most interesting is St Peter's church (1888) at Pentre. The mountain road up to Pen-rhys passes Ffynnon Fair, a holy well associated with the site (no visible remains) of a medieval Franciscan monastery.

RHOSILI

Rhosili stands high up on the cliff edge overlooking a 3 mile (5 km) stretch of sandy beach, reached by a steep and winding footpath, which is one of the finest in Britain. The tiny village has a gable-towered church (see chapter 5). Remains of an earlier church and a medieval settlement have been found nearer the beach in excavations at the Warren (see chapter 3). The spectacular coastline includes the serpent-like island of Worms Head to the south-west; the island is connected to the rocky mainland by a neck of rock known as the Devil's Bridge but is only accessible at low tide. On the southern coastline of the parish there are iron age promontory forts at The Knave and Thurba Head (see chapter 3).

RHYMNEY (Rhymni)

Rhymney stands near the source of the river of the same name and developed as an ironmaking town based on the Upper Furnace Ironworks established in 1800 at Blaenrhymni. The Bute Ironworks of 1827, lower down the valley, had a blast-furnace designed to look like an Egyptian temple. The Bute Company Shop gained notoriety during the nineteenth century because of its continuance of the truck system (whereby workmen were paid in goods instead of cash) some 54 years after the 1831 Anti-Truck Act had officially abolished the practice. The pseudo-classical church of St David (see chapter 5) is worth a visit. Butetown, originally known as Y Drenewydd, at the head of the valley, is an interesting example of early town planning (see chapter 8).

SWANSEA (Abertawe)
Early closing Thursday; market days Monday to Friday.

Swansea is the second largest town both in Glamorgan and in Wales. Lying at the mouth of the Tawe river, it was once the metallurgical capital of the world and is still busy with industry. But Swansea is a city of contrasts, where industry and tourism compete and survive almost side by side, and where the valleys meet the culturally and physically different Gower peninsula. As a seaside resort Swansea's great attraction is the miles of safe sandy beach fringing the beautiful curving coastline of Swansea Bay and ending at Mumbles Head.

Although the name Swansea, meaning 'Sweyn's island', is probably of Viking origin there appears to have been no town until the Normans arrived. The first castle (see chapter 4) was built in the early twelfth century by the Earl of Warwick as the headquarters of his newly won lordship of Gower. The remains of the castle which are now visible date from a later rebuilding. The town's first charter was given by a later Earl sometime between 1153 and 1184. Following the Act of Union in the sixteenth century the lordship of Gower was united with the old lordship of Glamorgan (Morgannwg) to form the new Tudor county of Glamorgan.

Swansea's industrial growth began in the early eighteenth century with the development of the copper-smelting industry, using ores imported from Anglesey and Cornwall. By the end of the eighteenth century the first Harbour Act had been obtained and the Swansea Canal, linking the port with the Tawe valley, was constructed in 1798. The Oystermouth Railway (later known as the Mumbles Railway) was opened in 1807 and a

second canal (the Tennant) was constructed between 1821 and 1824. The South Wales Railway reached Swansea in 1850 and two years later the first dock was opened. By the middle of the nineteenth century more than half of all British copper works were located in or near Swansea. By the end of the century Swansea was also the main centre in Britain for the production of tinplate and zinc, while other smelting industries included lead, silver, cobalt, gold and nickel. When the industries eventually closed they left behind them a desert of dereliction which remained until the area was reclaimed and partly forested in the 1970s and 1980s as part of the Lower Swansea Valley Project. Fortunately for those interested in industrial archaeology, a number of industrial relics still survive in various parts of the city (see chapter 8).

For a brief period during the nineteenth century Swansea was also famous for its fine porcelain ware. Previously china had been made at the Cambrian Pottery. Then in 1814 Lewis Weston Dillwyn took over the pottery and started producing porcelain. The beautifully decorated work produced during this period is comparable with the best porcelain in Europe but, unfortunately, the soft paste had certain peculiarities which made it difficult to manufacture successfully and the production of Swansea porcelain ceased in 1824.

Swansea suffered heavily from enemy action during the Second World War. Much of the town centre was destroyed by bombing and has since been rebuilt. One victim of the blitz was St Mary's church (rebuilt by Sir Arthur Blomfield in 1898). Another was the home of the remarkable 'Beau' Nash (see chapter 10) in College Street. Fortunately the Glynn Vivian Art Gallery (see chapter 7) in Alexandra Road and the museum in the Royal Institution of South Wales (see chapter 7), near the docks, survived. The Maritime Museum (see chapter 7), in the Maritime Quarter facing the South Dock, is a more recent creation. As part of the ambitious redevelopment of the Maritime Quarter the South Dock has been transformed into a marina and contains a reconstructed man-of-war, the *Picton Sea Eagle*.

Also in the docks area is the old Guildhall, built in 1852 to designs by Thomas Taylor and later used as a school. A new Guildhall, designed in smooth neo-classical style by Sir Percy Thomas, was built in 1934 a mile (1.6 km) from the town centre. From the outside its

chief feature is a 160 foot (49 metre) high rectangular clock-tower. The Brangwyn Hall inside houses sixteen panels commemorating the British Empire, painted by Sir Frank Brangwyn. Originally intended for the House of Lords in London, they were considered to be too controversial for that institution. They now form a fine background to the Swansea Festival each autumn.

The Patti Pavilion in Victoria Park, just beyond the Guildhall, was brought from Craig-y-Nos Castle in Powys, where it once served as the Winter Garden for the Victorian opera star Adelina Patti. Nearby, in Cwmdonkin Park, there is a memorial to the poet Dylan Thomas (see chapter 10), who lived in this area as a child and described his native town as 'an ugly, lovely town ... crawling, sprawling, slummed, unplanned, jerry-villa'd and smug-suburbed by the side of a long and splendid shore'.

Further along the 'splendid shore' are the University College of Swansea, established in 1920 around Singleton Abbey (built in 1826), and **Oystermouth** with its castle (see chapter 4). Thomas Bowdler (see chapter 10), the censor of Shakespeare, is buried in Oystermouth church. **Mumbles Head**, at the furthest tip of Swansea Bay, has a pier and a lifeboat station and on a nearby rocky islet there is a lighthouse dating from 1784.

Swansea: the clock-tower of the Guildhall.

13
Tourist information centres

Aberdulais: *Aberdulais Basin, Aberdulais, near Neath SA10 8ED. Telephone: 0639 633531.
Baglan: *Beefeater Restaurant, Sunnycroft Road, Baglan SA12 8DS. Telephone: 0639 823049.
Barry Island: *The Promenade, Barry Island CF6 8TJ. Telephone: 0446 747171.
Caerphilly: *Old Police Station, Park Lane, Caerphilly CF18 1AA. Telephone: 0222 851378.
Cardiff: 8-14 Bridge Street, Cardiff CF1 2EE. Telephone: 0222 227281.
Merthyr Tydfil: 14a Glebeland Street, Merthyr Tydfil CF47 8AU. Telephone: 0685 79884.
Mumbles: *Oystermouth Square, Mumbles SA3 4DQ. Telephone: 0792 361302.
Pontypridd: Pontypridd Historical Centre, Bridge Street, Pontypridd CF37 3PE.
Porthcawl: *Old Police Station, John Street, Porthcawl CF36 3DT. Telephone: 0656 716639.
Sarn: Sarn Park Service Area, Junction 36, M4 Motorway, Sarn, near Bridgend CF32 9SY.
  Telephone: 0656 654906.
Swansea: Singleton Street, Swansea SA1 3QN. Telephone: 0792 468321.

* Seasonal opening.

The cottage at Oxwich where John Wesley stayed when on his preaching tour of the Gower peninsula.

GLAMORGAN

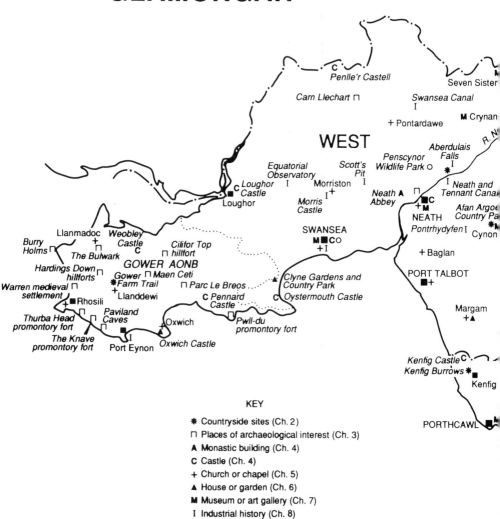

C Penlle'r Castell

Seven Sister

Carn Llechart □

Swansea Canal
I

M Crynan

+ Pontardawe

R. N

WEST

Aberdulais
Falls

Penscynor
Wildlife Park O

Equatorial
Observatory

Scott's
Pit

Morriston   I

Loughor
C Castle

Loughor

Morris
Castle

I+

Neath **A**
Abbey   □
I

+ **■C**
M

I Neath and
Tennant Canal

Afan Argoe
Country Pa

NEATH

Pontrhydyfen I

Cynon

SWANSEA
M■CO
+I

+ Baglan

Llanmadoc   Weobley
+   Castle

Cilifor Top
□ hillfort

PORT TALBOT
■+

Burry
Holms   The Bulwark   C

GOWER AONB

Hardings Down □
hillforts

Gower □ Maen Ceti

Margam
+▲

Warren medieval □
settlement

✳Farm Trail
+

Llanddewi

□ Parc Le Breos

Clyne Gardens and
▲ Country Park

C Oystermouth Castle

■ Rhosili

Paviland
Caves

C Pennard
Castle

Kenfig Castle C

Thurba Head □
promontory fort

Oxwich
□

□ Pwll-du
promontory fort

Kenfig Burrows ✳
■

The Knave
promontory fort

I
Port Eynon Oxwich Castle

Kenfig

PORTHCAWL

KEY

✳ Countryside sites (Ch. 2)
□ Places of archaeological interest (Ch. 3)
A Monastic building (Ch. 4)
C Castle (Ch. 4)
+ Church or chapel (Ch. 5)
▲ House or garden (Ch. 6)
M Museum or art gallery (Ch. 7)
I Industrial history (Ch. 8)
O Other places to visit (Ch. 9)
■ Town or village (Ch. 12)

BRECON BEACONS
NATIONAL PARK

Morlais
Castle
C
Butetown
I
Brecon Mountain O
Railway
Cyfarthfa Castle ▲
I **M**
+ ■ **MERTHYR
TYDFIL**
+ ■ RHYMNEY

Craig y Llyn
hill walk
*
Dare Valley
Country Park
Parc Cwm
* Darran
* I
Cwm Dare
Industrial Trail
■ I **ABERDARE**
New I
Tredegar
Carn
Bugail ┌┐
ed Morgannwg
ay
Glamorgan
Canal I
Stuart Crystal
Glassworks ○
**MOUNTAIN
ASH** ■
BARGOED ■
Gelligaer ●
Penydarren
Tramroad I
▲ Llancaiach-
fawr
■ RHONDDA
Hengoed I
Viaduct

MID

Rhondda Heritage I
Park
I
PONTYPRIDD
R. Taff / Afon Taf
○
Old Mill Forge and
Melin Ystrad

ESTEG
+ I
Gilfach Goch I
Industrial Trail
Machen Forge I
Industrial Trail
C ■ **CAERPHILLY**

* Bryngarw
Country Park
LLANTRISANT
+ ■○ Ridgeway *
Walk
* Three Castles
Cycle Route
▲ Castell
Coch
* I Glamorgan Canal
Nature Reserve

astle
astle
+
C Coity
C
C

astle
astle
■ **C** ■
BRIDGEND
Hensol Forest *
St Fagans **M**
Castle ▲
+**C**
Llandaf
CARDIFF
┌┐ +
■ **C** ■ **M**
○ I
yr
■ +
○ + Ewenny
C Ogmore Castle
dleston
tle
SOUTH
┌┐ Caerau
hillfort

)┌┐
aven
ontory fort
C +○
COWBRIDGE
Tinkinswood ┌┐
Llandough
Dyffryn ▲
Gardens
Maes-y-
┌┐ felin
Cogan
+
Beaupre Castle ▲
Dinas Powys **C**
Castle
■ **M** +**PENARTH**
Llancarfan
■ +
○ Welsh
Hawking Centre
┌┐ * Cosmeston
Lakes

Nash ┌┐
tory fort
St Donat's
I
**LLANTWIT
MAJOR** ■
Porthkerry Country
Park
BARRY
*
ash Point
ighthouse
St Donat's
Castle
+
Summerhouse Camp
┌┐ promontory fort
M
Rhoose Glan-y-Mor
Sully Island

ORGAN HERITAGE COAST
I *●
Flat Holm

Index

Page numbers in italics refer to illustrations.

Aberbargoed 55
Aberdare 66-7
  Cwm Dare Industrial Trail 46-7
  Dare Valley Country Park 8-9
  Robertstown Tramroad Bridge 47
Aberdulais 6, 7, 47
Afan Argoed Country Park 7
Atlantic College 40
Baglan 26
Bargoed 67
Barry 12, 67
  Glan-y-Mor Roman site 15
  Welsh Hawking Centre 57
Beaupre Castle *35*, 35-6
Bishopton Valley 10
Bowdler, Thomas 58
Brecon Beacons National Park 7-8
Brecon Mountain Railway 55, *56*
Bridgend 26-7, 67
  Newcastle 23
Bryngarw Country Park 8
Bulwark, The 13
Burry Holms 13
Bute family 58
Butetown (Cardiff) 64-5
Butetown (Rhymney) 52
Button, Sir Thomas 58
Caerau hillfort 14
Caerphilly 67
  Castle 4, *18*, 18-19
Candleston Castle 20
Caradog 13
Cardiff 4, 5, 6, *63*, 63-5, *64*, *65*
  Bute Road Railway Station 47
  Caerau hillfort 14
  Castle 4, 14, *19*, 20-1
  churches 27
  Melingriffith water pump 48
  museums 41-2
  Old Pumping Station 47
  Roman fort 4, *13*, 14
  Techniquest 57
  See also under Llandaf
Carn Bugail burial chamber 14
Carn Llechart burial chamber 14
Castell Coch *36*, 36-7
Cefn Coed Colliery Museum 42
Cefn Viaduct 49, *49*
Cilifor Top hillfort *12*, 14-15
Claypits Pottery 55
Coed Morgannwg Way 8
Cogan 27-8
Coity 28
  Castle 21
Cosmeston Lakes Country Park 8

medieval village *14*, 15
Cowbridge 28, 55, *66*, 68
  Porth Melin *24*, 25
Craig y Llyn *6*, 8
Crawshay family 58
Crynant 42
Cwm Dare Industrial Trail 46-7
Cyfarthfa Castle 37, *37*, 43
Cyfarthfa Ironworks 49
Cynonville 42
Dare Valley Country Park 8-9
Dillwyn-Llewelyn, John 59
Dinas Powys Castle 21
Dowlais Ironworks 49
Dunraven Park 10
  promontory fort 15
Dyffryn Gardens 37-8, *38*
Edwards, William 59
Elliott Colliery Winding House 50-1
Equatorial Observatory 52
Ewenny Priory 5, *28*, 28-9
  potteries 55
Flat Holm 9, 47
Garwnant Forest 8
Gelligaer 68
Gilfach Goch Industrial Trail 47
Glamorgan Canal Nature Reserve 9, 12
Glamorgan Heritage Coast 9-10
Glamorganshire Canal 48
Glan-y-Mor Roman site 15
Gower A O N B 3, 10-11
Gower Farm Museum 11, *11*
Guest, Sir Josiah and Lady 59
Hardings Down hillforts 15
Hatton, Julia Ann 59
Hengoed Viaduct 48, *48*
Hensol Forest 11
Ilston 5
James, Evan and James 59
Kenfig 68
  Burrows 11
  Castle 11, 21
Lavernock 72
Lewis, Alun 59
Llancaiach-fawr 38
Llancarfan 4, 29, 68-9
Llandaf 65
  Bishop's Castle 18
  Cathedral *29*, 29-30, *30*
Llanddewi 30-1
Llandough 4, *30*, 31
Llangennith 5
Llanmadoc 31
Llantrisant 12, 31, 55, 69
Llantwit Major 4, 31, *31*, 69
Llynfi Ironworks 48
Loughor 69
  Castle 4, 21

Machen Forge Industrial Trail 48
Maen Ceti burial chamber 15
Maesteg 48, 70
Maes-y-felin burial chamber 15, *16*
Margam Abbey 5, 31-2
  Orangery 39, *39*
  Park 38-9
  Stones Museum 32
Melin Ystrad 55
Merthyr Mawr 32, 70
  bridge *1*
  Warren 10
Merthyr Tydfil 6, 70-1
  Cefn Viaduct 49
  church 32
  Cyfartha Castle 37, *37*
  Cyfarthfa Ironworks 49
  Dowlais Ironworks 49
  Morlais Castle 22
  Penydarren Tramroad 50
  Ynysfach Engine House 50
Morgan, Griffith 60
Morgannwg, Iolo (Edward Williams) 60
Morriston 32, 54
Mountain Ash 71
Nash, Richard 'Beau' 60
Nash Point Lighthouse 50
Nash promontory fort 15, *16*
National Museum of Wales 41, *41*
Neath 6, 71-2
  Abbey 5, *22*, 22-3
  Canal 50
  Castle 4, 23
  church 32
  museum 43
  Roman fort 4, 15
New Tredegar *3*
  Elliott Colliery Winding House 50
Novello, Ivor 60
Nyth-bran, Guto (Griffith Morgan) 60
Ogmore Castle 4, *23*, 23-4
Oxwich 32
  Burrows 10
  Castle 39
Oystermouth 76
Parc Cwm Darran 12
Parc Le Breos burial chamber 14
Parry, Joseph 60
Paviland Caves 16
Penarth 32-3, *33*, *71*, 72
  Cosmeston Lakes Country Park 8
  Turner House Art Gallery 43
Penlle'r Castell 24
Pennard Castle *2*, 24
Penscynor Wildlife Park 55
Penydarren Tramroad 50
Pontardawe 33

Pontrhydyfen 51, *51*
Pontypridd 33, *72*, 72-3
  Hen Bont 51, *52*
Port Eynon 10, 51-2, *53*, 73
Porth 52
Porthcawl 73
  museum 43
Porthkerry Country Park 12
Port Talbot 26, 33, 73
Price, Richard 61
Price, William *60*, 61
Prichard, John 61
Pwll-du promontory fort 17
Rhondda 73-4
  Heritage Park 52, *53*
  Valley 4
Rhosili 10, *10*, 11, 17, 33, 74
Rhymney 33, 52, 74-5
Richards, Ceri 61
Ridgeway Walk 12
Roberts, Evan 61
Robertstown Tramroad Bridge *46*, 47
St Donat's *9*
  Castle 39-40
St Fagans 40, *40*, 43-4
Sully Island 12
Summerhouse Camp promontory fort 17
Swansea 5, 6, 75-6, *76*
  Canal 54
  Castle 4, 25, *25*
  churches 32, 34
  Clyne Gardens 37
  Equatorial Observatory 52-3
  Morris Castle 54
  museums 44-5, *45*
  Plantasia 55, *57*
  Scott's Pit 54, *54*
  Tabernacle Chapel 32
Oystermouth Castle 24
Taf Vale Railway 6
Thomas, Dylan 62
Three Castles Cycle Route 12
Three Cliffs Bay 7, 10
Thurba Head promontory fort 17
Tinkinswood burial chamber 17, *17*
Wales Aircraft Museum 43
Warren medieval settlement 17
Welch Regiment Museum 42
Welsh Folk Museum 43-4, *44*
Welsh Hawking Centre 57
Welsh Industrial and Maritime Museum 42, *42*
Welsh Miners Museum 42
Weobley Castle 25
Whitford Burrows 11
Williams, Edward 62
Ynysfach Engine House 50
Ystrad Mynach 55